Foreword by [

LEGITIMIZING
THE NEW HUSTLE

Creating People-First Workplaces

MICHELE FELTES, MA

Legitimizing the New Hustle:
Creating People-First Workplaces
© 2024 People First Workplaces

The contents of this book are for educational and entertainment purposes only.

First published by Creative Services International, Inc.

Printed in the United States of America
Creative Services International, Inc.
2615 George Busbee Pkwy
Suite 11-154
Kennesaw, GA 30144-4981

csicorporation.com

Book and Cover design by CSI, Inc
WCL graphic designed by Coté Soerens

Table of Contents

Dedication

I dedicate this book to my husband Dean Feltes who is the love of my life and has been for 41 years. I also dedicate this book to my children and their families, to my extended family (you know who you are), to the One City United team, and to all those who have overcome barriers and are thriving because you invested in yourselves. You have given this white church lady understanding, grace, time, and the patience needed to change my perceptions, perspectives, and prejudices. You taught me the importance of using my voice for advocacy. You are my heroes! Thank you for trusting the process.

~ Michele Feltes

Leroy Cannon was my neighbor who had returned from prison and fell through the cracks. He had no opportunities to successfully return home. During his time in prison, he researched ways to develop nonprofits and businesses but never had the resources. I would walk my dog and see Leroy sitting outside, two houses down from my house. He would sometimes be hanging out with friends and drinking most of the time. It wasn't until the last years of his life that Leroy was able to address his lifetime of trauma. Leroy did not know it but he became part of my reason for doing the work I do and an inspiration for developing One City United. I remember a service provider (social worker by trade) who worked for Black Hawk Grundy Mental Health reaching out to me and sharing "Leroy's childhood traumas are the worst I have ever heard. I cried with him." When Leroy got the services he needed, life changed. It took years for this to happen. Literally years... But Leroy had to be ready. I had the honor of witnessing his change. He became my biggest cheerleader. Unfortunately, Leroy never got to see the work we do at One City United. I give Leroy Cannon, a true survivor, an honorarium of being my true heartfelt inspiration for this book. All lives can change!

~ The White Church Lady aka Michele

Foreword
by David Shapiro

The book you're about to dive into, *Legitimizing the New Hustle: Creating People First Workplaces*, is a powerful manifesto for a new way of thinking about work, community, and the responsibilities we share as leaders. It is timely, and I am honored to contribute a few thoughts to set the stage.

As someone who has spent years building inclusive workplaces and advocating for Total Worker Health®, I've seen firsthand how our workplace cultures can uplift or undermine our people. My work with the Centers for Health, Work & Environment at the Colorado School of Public Health has given me a front-row seat to the transformation happening across industries, where employers prioritize well-being, equity, and the long-term success of their people.

This book resonates deeply with my mission of fostering healthy, supportive workplaces that treat employees not just as workers but as whole individuals, especially those facing challenges like recovery, mental health issues, or re-entry from carceral settings.

We find ourselves in a pivotal moment where workplaces must evolve, or risk becoming obsolete. The urgency is palpable: across industries, leaders are grappling with burnout, talent retention, and the need to make work more human, all while adapting to rapid technological changes.

The pandemic and the Great Resignation have only magnified these challenges, forcing organizations to confront the harsh reality that the old ways of working no longer work. Now, more than ever, we need frameworks like the ones presented in this book to lead us toward sustainable, inclusive solutions.

Legitimizing the New Hustle is more than just a guide; it's a roadmap for the future of work. It's a celebration of companies like *Community Bank & Trust, Western Home Communities, Kay Park and Recreation, and UnityPoint Health* that are breaking down barriers and creating People First Workplaces. These businesses embrace innovative hiring practices, support minoritized employees, and foster inclusive cultures that produce tangible results.

- **Community Bank & Trust** offers financial stability programs to help Momentum initiative graduates and community members build solid financial foundations, such as emergency savings accounts.
- **Western Home Communities** provides apprenticeship programs and career paths in healthcare, ensuring individuals can grow personally and professionally in a values-driven environment.
- **Kay Park and Recreation** is a multi-generational business dedicated to creating a People First culture. By partnering with Momentum, Kay Park broadens its hiring practices to reach people with potential, reinforcing their belief in assuming good intent and prioritizing their team's well-being over business demands.
- **UnityPoint Health - Waterloo** leads by example with inclusive hiring, offering internships to individuals with developmental disabilities, and demonstrating how workplaces can empower people of all backgrounds.

These examples showcase the power of inclusion and how breaking long-held stigmas—whether related to mental health, recovery, or re-entry—leads to more robust, resilient organizations.

The heart of this book emphasizes that it's the person, not the background, we should consider. The participants of *One City United's Momentum* program are a testament to this mindset. Many have transformed their lives by turning their experiences into strengths, gaining meaningful employment, and creating brighter futures for themselves and their families.

The story of Legitimizing the New Hustle is, at its heart, one of hope, resilience, and transformation. It's about creating workplaces where individuals are seen and supported in their journey of self-actualization; where their stories of overcoming are valued as a source of strength, not shame.

This book invites us to reimagine our workplaces as communities that foster personal and professional growth. It's an inspiring call to action for employers, leaders, or community advocates to create workplaces that put people first. In any line of work, any company, new or old, can benefit from seeing people for their potential, instead of their past.

I invite you to read on and discover the compelling vision of People First Workplaces—a vision that, if we embrace it, has the power to reshape not just how we work but also how we live and connect as a society. This vision is not just a possibility, but a call to action, inspiring us to create workplaces that truly put people first.

Introduction

My husband, Dean, and I have always challenged the status quo; as a couple and as determined nonprofit leaders. Rather than accepting limitations, we ask, 'Why not?' instead of 'Why?' Our mission is to create People First Workplaces, that break down employment stigmas and help marginalized individuals find fulfilling, self-sustaining jobs across various industries.

This is what *Legitimizing The New Hustle: Creating People-First Workplaces* is about.

These companies are change makers, breaking the stigmas, and promoting growth strategies for employees within their own communities and organizations. We are proud to present this collaborative book. Four businesses, along with their leadership, have contributed chapters, each identifying the People-First vision needed to overcome long-held human resource policies and engage in intentional change-making strategies.

They're not just talking about it - they're doing the work. Their impact on our community has been incredibly positive, in ways that will affect generations to come, by legitimizing this new approach and Creating People First Workplaces.

> This is what Legitimizing The New Hustle: Creating People-First Workplaces is about.

We invite you to enjoy and celebrate these employers and their staff - individuals who have overcome barriers and adversities. We'd like to thank:

- **Community Bank & Trust President, Stacey Bentley,** for giving a President's Perspective. Your impact is forever imprinted on the lives and families of the Cedar Valley.
- **Chris & Larry Borglum, Co-Owners of Kay Park and Recreation,** a multi-generational business in Janesville, Iowa, and his Operations Manager, Schad West, who thinks outside the box and challenges the status quo to put people first.

- **UnityPoint Health Waterloo's team, including Kingsley Botchway II, the Regional Director of Human Resources,** and all the amazing leaders who hire according to strengths, assets, and abilities.
- **Western Home Communities' CEO Kris Hansen and COO Darrell McCormick,** who have taken creating community very seriously and developed educational models that we should all embrace.

Thank you all for your contributions and commitment to creating People-First workplaces!

We were blessed with the grit to take on this challenging work for such a time as this. We are also blessed to have the buy-in of other prominent organizations who also understand and are doing the work.

Our company, *One City United,* was born from over five years of research and development conducted in underserved neighborhoods in Waterloo, IA. Our research led us to identify needs, or gaps, that drove us to find solutions to equip people. We collaborate with businesses, organizations, churches, and individuals to identify needs and develop programs that promote life transformation, fresh opportunities, and lasting economic and social ripple effects.

Under *One City's Momentum Employment* program, we offer life-transforming education that focuses on the end goal: placing people into positions that match their values. As co-founders of One City United in Waterloo, Iowa, we've been able to teach, train, and equip not only the participants of Momentum but also countless employers and organizations.

Our consulting services focus on breaking the stigmas related to mental health, recovery, and re-entry. In the workplace we emphasize personal leadership with staff who were once marginalized, as well as directly educating long-time valued employees who may need to learn and embrace a changing workplace culture.

We believe it's crucial that companies don't "go it alone" in this work. The old ways of doing business still resonate strongly in our society today. It takes grit and compassion to guard the vision of changing culture, even when it gets hard and people tell you it won't work.

To lead means to be a change agent. We help companies grow and transform their business culture while re-humanizing employment.

Our goal is to help organizations better understand ways to embrace change and serve their employees by setting up systems of success that will impact generations.

At **One City United**, our executive staff and collaborators guide individuals, groups, and corporations in better understanding the barriers faced by marginalized populations. We often hear, "I want to change my hiring practices and be more inclusive because I'm missing out on great people." We agree. You are.

Supporting your current staff can be challenging. We assist leaders in developing a deeper understanding of related stigmas and the neighborhoods within their organizational reach for employment. Recruiting individuals isn't usually the problem - you probably already have great staff. We believe that we all need to start in our own backyards (our companies) and support our current employees. We teach you how to do both: support existing staff and recruit inclusively.

We teach you how to do both: support existing staff and recruit inclusively.

The organizational connections we're networking with at One City United are creating real change. We aim to help you create people-first workplaces that contribute to your (ROI) return on investment. It's always better to retain quality, educated staff who create a positive culture within your organization.

We assist in disrupting outdated recruitment practices and offer opportunities to teach, train, and equip a quality workforce. We focus on challenging the status quo in your culture and ending long-held stigmas. We all have them, and they usually need to be disrupted.

Our approach may involve re-establishing productive communication strategies, creating problem-solving protocols, and identifying how to measure effective company transformation. This all takes buy-in from your respective communities. Yes, I said communities - if you desire to have a cohesive workplace, you have to have a community. Individuals spend a majority of their lives at work, so community matters.

Sometimes it takes getting rid of the "NIMBY" (Not In My Back Yard) attitudes. We explore how employment is like a puzzle, and we are all crucial pieces who are necessary for its completion. Our corporate education on health, safety, and recovery-first employment means we connect and consult to support your staff. We teach, train, and equip them to look at possibilities, asking "What if?" and "What does that look like?"

One City United offers support through peer coaching individually and with a cohort model for employers and their staff. We look forward to you joining us in this journey to Create People-First Workplaces.

The names of class participants, graduates of Momentum have been changed for privacy purposes.

When you look for the bad in mankind,
expecting to find it, you surely will.

~ Abraham Lincoln

CHAPTER ONE

The Problem

I always thought the job of a Human Resource Director was to hire talent. Then I was informed at a mock interview, by a retired HR professional, that many Human Resource professionals are trained to eliminate risk.

When a business starts with fear-based ideologies how does anyone have a chance of gaining successful employment?

I once read if you want to understand the entrepreneur, you should study the juvenile delinquent. (MacLellan) Wow... It's because the entrepreneur challenges the status quo. So does the juvenile delinquent. Isn't that ironic?

The bottom line is by not hiring people due to stigmas; re-entry, recovery, and mental health, employers are missing out on excellent problem solvers. Entrepreneurs possess "think outside the box" mindsets. Those mindsets, coupled with natural survival skills, showcase their insights on how to read others.

My passion for working with individuals in employment began during my time as a healthcare consultant. As a non-nurse consultant, I was the first to arrive at the building each week, and I would stay until the very end, often for a significant period, to ensure all problems were resolved. I remained on site until the state's final inspection confirmed that all compliance issues had been adequately addressed. If there were any lingering problems, I made sure they would be identified during the inspection.

This was an experience that improved my understanding as to why it is so important to love your job. I also learned more than I wanted to know about what toxic workplaces could look like.

When I found a problem, I reported it and gave recommendations as to how staff needed to change practices and policies.

I did not love my job. My job security was based on others not meeting expectations, not completing tasks correctly, and ultimately failing their job. In that position, I realized the importance of great leadership that sees value in soft skills, training, and professional development of their staff.

As I reflect on that experience, I realize there are parallels between the strict perspectives of those hiring managers and their unwillingness to push back on flawed company policies, even when doing so could improve the organization.

Many hiring managers get stuck looking so deeply into a candidate's past that they miss qualified and talented individuals who are resilient and can narrate their stories of overcoming, life transformation, and transforming their lives.

Companies can often overlook the beauty in an individual overcoming and surviving challenges and then humbling themselves by changing their narrative and becoming lifelong learners. As a result of analysis paralysis from hearing or seeing these three stigma-inducing words; "Felony", "Mental Health," or "Recovery," hiring managers can discount the transformational narrative that worthy individuals tell.

 Many hiring managers get stuck looking so deeply into a candidate's past that they miss qualified and talented individuals . . .

WHAT ARE STIGMAS?

Definition: a mark of disgrace associated with a particular circumstance, quality, or person. Here's an example statement someone might say, "The stigma of having gone to prison will always be with me."

Stigmas can be narratives (stories) we create in our mind concerning someone's past experiences whether it be mental health, recovery, or re-entry. Truth be told, many of us have circumstances in our past we are not proud of and that we wish we could change.

America incarcerates more people than any other country in the world. Mass incarceration is affecting the whole pie. (Wagner) Now it has impacted not only the micro (the families) it has affected the macro (the workforce).

I believe it will be the employers that will engage the socioeconomics of what these stigmas do within the workforce, changing the narrative by creating inclusive and people-first workplaces. By rehumanizing employment, companies are challenging the status quo, starting from within and moving to the state and national platforms with their message: "Re-humanize Employment."

To rehumanize employment I must first address dehumanization. I want you to know that at *One City United* we focus on solutions. We are a solution-based organization. It is important to us that we assist professionals in better understanding the impact of policies. In my opinion, it correlates directly and indirectly to the results we are all seeing in employment today. This is where perspective comes into the conversation.

When researching to write this book, the term rehumanizing employment came to me while listening to *Audible* and reading Brene' Brown's books. Yes, I am a fan. I started to really become interested in Brene's work prior, but more so after she started to work with Eric Mosley from Work Human. Brene' interviewed Eric on her podcast in an episode called "Brene' with Eric Mosley on *Making Work Human."* She quoted Eric inquisitively, pondering, "You say that work might be the last best place to realize our full humanity." His answer revolves around where people give their trust. There has been a culture shift to trust in the workplace. People today trust their workplaces more than the church and the government. (Brown and Mosley) I find that to be very good news for employers. This inspires and engages me in my research because in our work at One City's *Momentum* we start by questioning and teaching, "What is the foundation of all good relationships?

The answer is: Trust. Employment is a relationship. All companies want is to trust you." All employees want is to trust their employer.

I knew what I wanted to communicate but did not have a name for it. Through Brown's books I realized what we need to do in America related to our workforce is to rehumanize it. Change the status quo for employment and create people-first workplaces. In Brene's book, *Atlas Of The Heart, Mapping Meaningful Connection and the Language of Human Experience* she states, "Dehumanization continues to be one of the greatest threats to humanity." She shares that dehumanization is

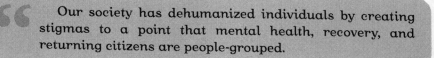

> Our society has dehumanized individuals by creating stigmas to a point that mental health, recovery, and returning citizens are people-grouped.

a process. Brown cites the work of Michelle Maiese, a professor in the philosophy department at Emmanuel College, on how this all works. She shares that it always starts with language. I will add rhetoric which can make a people group seem less-than or not-worthy-of. In the Momentum Employment program at One City United, we track how people are noticing and choosing their thoughts throughout the six weeks. Worthiness related to employment can be a huge beast that, once transformation begins, becomes a beautiful thing in *One City's Momentum* classes. At times, the perceived barriers are as challenging and difficult to overcome as the very real ones.

Our society has dehumanized individuals by creating stigmas to a point that mental health, recovery, and returning citizens are peoplegrouped. I don't want to give dehumanization much time in this book, but I want to address it. If you are truly going to create a people first workplace, language matters.

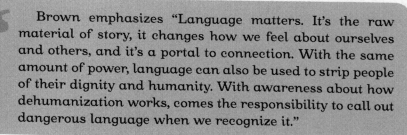

> Brown emphasizes "Language matters. It's the raw material of story, it changes how we feel about ourselves and others, and it's a portal to connection. With the same amount of power, language can also be used to strip people of their dignity and humanity. With awareness about how dehumanization works, comes the responsibility to call out dangerous language when we recognize it."

My response to business leaders is with the question, "How are you challenging the status quo?"

By turning business exclusion into seeking re-humanization in employment practices, we can focus on values and leadership, therefore developing a people-first model.

This model promotes a workforce that works in harmony, that can understand each other, and in turn, is no longer complacent but rather engaged because they are being understood. A positive and productive work environment is created when employees' personal values align with the values emphasized in their workplace, allowing them to feel fulfilled in their roles.

CHALLENGES & DREAMS

These challenges and dreams were shared with me in response to an Ideal Reader questionnaire given to the business leaders who contributed to this book. At One City United we are solution based. Knowing the challenges and problems is just the beginning to best understand the solutions. These were responses given by business leaders from Community Bank & Trust, Kay Park Recreation, Unity Point Hospital, and Western Home Communities. I wanted to better understand what makes their businesses stand out. The following are my very inquisitive questions to gather research on understanding the amazing leadership in the four contributing people-first workplaces in this book. Their responses were very insightful. You may be able to relate:

What is your biggest problem or frustration? - in your words.

- "We need better communication at every level. *Clear* is kind, and *understanding* is the key to empowerment. It's important that organizations work to communicate changes effectively to team members to ensure everyone knows the direction of the organization and how they can help." *(Botchway)*
- "Balancing diversity of thought with common values is how you turn a true "Vision" into reality. It is hard to get everyone rowing in the same direction if they all have different values. Identifying people who will buy into your values are the ones you want on your team. We can have common values, but because of the way people think about things, they tend to come at it from very different directions, each with a unique perspective. To a lot of people, this can sound like disagreement. If you are willing to question and listen to the intent, you will often see that

you are both trying to get to the same place. Together, with the consideration of more people being addressed and included, a diverse group will come up with better, more complete answers." *(Borglum)*

- "Your sphere of influence, no matter what it is perceived to be, it's still only about as far as you can physically reach. In other words, you still have to navigate inside of things that you can't control. A lot of times the leader is blamed for not being able to change those dynamics. You just have to be creative while operating inside of these guardrails." *(Hansen)*
- "Not sure "world," but in my world of banking, it is Communication- is making sure the right time, right place, and right team feel informed. It's helping us accept change as we move and grow. It's maintaining a positive, inclusive culture where everyone has a say, and together we create a common vision." *(Bentley)*

PROBLEMS FROM BUSINESS LEADERS' PERSPECTIVES

The following problems were shared with me. These are industry change - makers, who desire to keep up with how fast our society is advancing, changing, and transforming the model of work.

What are you most worried about?

- "Changing demographics and expectations within the workforce – Loss of Baby Boomer generation and new generation that has an entirely different expectation regarding careers, pay, schedule, benefits." *(West)*
- "I worry that our positive stories about giving team members second chances and leaning into having a more diverse and inclusive environment and workforce will get overshadowed by the negativity pervasive in the world today." *(Botchway)*

What keeps them up at night?

- "Talent acquisition and retention of our team. I worry about how to have engaged, diverse team members who have the same passion to assist/partner with our clients." *(Bentley)*
- "The mental health of our team members especially in the health care setting. They are doing amazing work caring for our patients and I worry they are not taking care of themselves. We

want to be an organization that takes care of all of our team members. We are working towards this goal, but we have some opportunities to do better. *(Botchway)*

- "Things that are beyond your direct control and how can you still do your best to influence outcomes? How can you try to better mitigate risk or influence positive outcomes?" (Hansen)
- "Very little and mostly my kids :) Market and census development, access to capital and workforce challenges that limit the services we can provide." *(McCormick)*

When business leaders are losing sleep, it can be positively life-altering for everyone who is impacted by their choices. There are many restless nights when the brain is overloaded, which can lead to ideas, concepts, innovation, and strategy. But how?

Strategy . . . With some assistance. A. Because not every leader is the key strategist, B. It can result in some of the biggest employment problems being solved.

That is the purpose of this book; to rehumanize employment and assist the leader to better understand they are not on an island alone.

There is help.

My dear friend, author and NGO leader, Annie Vander Werff has encouraged us to share our first-hand knowledge with business leaders because they want to understand how to engage the community as a whole and not marginalize it further.

Our goal is to help corporate leaders build healthy workplaces that embrace differences. We aim to achieve this by providing models focused on wellness dimensions, preparing individuals entering their preferred industry, and educating current and long-term staff to value diversity.

Annie added, "Due to changing demographics, mindsets, and competencies to understand, the previous generation is rarely qualified for this challenge."

Oh, and I might add, political rhetoric that distracts us all and it can bring innovative progress to a startling halt. Can I say, "Too many variables!" I chose to move forward anyway.

In a season of political ads and confusion, sometimes it is best to just shut out the noise. The government wants and encourages us in great ways to become more inclusive, or not, depending on which way the wind is blowing on a certain day.

As business leaders, let us put all that aside and seek to understand how change starts in *our* space. How can we advance, grow, and engage our current staff in embracing the new workforce by educating and seeking a sense of belonging for everyone? When we overcome these obstacles, the government can learn from us. They are missing out by not changing their hiring policies, practices, and procedures. Maybe that is the next book?

Where are you on the stages of change?

As co-founders of *One City United*, we noticed that when we encouraged people to engage in self-reflection and transformative thinking around change and growth, they began to aspire to more than just having a job.

An instrumental piece is not solely seeking change but understanding that vocation is only a small part of it. I believe when businesses start focusing on the dimensions of wellness for their staff, they will be healthier and more productive because of it. Embracing the dimensions of wellness can change the trajectory of an individual's life. *(Stoewen)*

We witness it every term of Momentum with many ah ha moments as participants realize what they have been missing and realize where they became stuck. Debbie Stoewen said it best, "The past is history; the present and future lie in the choices you make today. Don't worry about getting it perfect; just get it going, and become the best kind of person you can be."

PEOPLE CAN CHANGE

This is related to business, and I am going to give you some backstory into my life so you can better understand how both Dean and I were given the passion to embrace the words "Change" and "Transformation."

As you read on, consider your own story of evolving, and your business transforming. In other words, why do you do what you do, and lead how you lead?

Thank God. First and foremost, I want to thank God because if I had not come to understand that people can change, I would not have been given the blessings of knowing so many extraordinary individuals.

But first, I had to understand that I could change.

This is one reason I know that people can change if given the opportunity. I was one of those people that needed to change. Since my change, the term "Those People" really gives me a feeling that emphasizes a sense of sadness in me, as I consider power structures that feed ethnocentric viewpoints, hurtful speech, and behavior that does not benefit anyone.

My mom taught me to seek the best and pray for the rest. That golden rule that people were taught for years, but many of us don't follow. I am sure I gave my mom a lot of practical applications in looking for the best and praying for the rest. I know I did. I may have been given all kinds of privilege growing up in rural Iowa, by loving parents who, of course, had their flaws and challenges.

I lived a very sheltered life. I enjoyed summers in 4-H, showing cattle at the county fairs, having a few close friends over, and just getting to be a kid. I had no diversity to speak of in my life until I moved from my Mayberry-style life in small-town Iowa to the "big city" of Waterloo.

In Waterloo, I began to realize I had some predisposed mindsets that I needed to lose. After living such a sheltered life there was so much, I needed to learn. I viewed life as I did because of how I was raised and how we raised our children. I had never even heard the term *White privilege* until a Black non-profit leader said to me, "You don't even know what White privilege is, do you?" I did not.

I was way too embarrassed to admit it, but I didn't know what it meant. I took it as an offensive term at first until I researched it and realized I did have it. I was privileged not to have to even know what this term meant.

I bring all my weaknesses to the non-profit One City United and I have to remind myself that vulnerability is a strength. We try to teach our participants, staff, and past graduates this too.

CHANGE IS INEVITABLE

Every term of Momentum is different from the next. One City United became a non-profit in 2018 and launched Momentum Urban Employment as a program in 2020. It is much like the workforce. It is designed to mimic the workplace because we all have stuff in life that we carry into our places of employment. The difference is we are no longer living in a Beaver Cleaver world of the fifties. The pandemic may have seemed like a curse for so many, but the one thing it did was align individuals' priorities, no matter what socio-economic status people were in. For those with little, it made their financials worse but their desire for what would meet their needs and fulfill their lives increased. It is now several years past the pandemic, and our world has had many changes.

We choose what we let into our space. Sometimes.

For those living in generational poverty, it can seem increasingly much more limited. Many times, the people we serve do not have access to the internet, phones, or computers. But these "badasses" always look for a way forward.

Graduates from previous terms often attend Momentum graduation ceremonies to support the new graduates, bonding through their shared

> Many times, the people we serve do not have access to the internet, phones, or computers. But these "badasses" always look for a way forward.

understanding of the effort required to complete the program.

One particular graduation day started with me receiving texts in the morning from grads who could not attend. I thought, "How thoughtful." At the graduation, the classroom coordinator told me, "I have got this all handled."

I was impressed and just sat back and enjoyed how each graduate shared the life changes they had made since beginning the six-week journey of Momentum. Several people gave me gift bags, which confused me. I was humbled when the classroom coordinator acknowledged me. She was the student who had become the teacher. All the graduates in attendance (Term 1-16) stood up and then they lined up, each presenting me with a rose. I greatly appreciated the recognition by the staff and all the graduates. I was overwhelmed and greatly humbled. But what each of these roses represented to me is that people CAN change. When given opportunities and the encouragement to believe in themselves again, they do things that give me great joy because they do things like enrolling in college.

At this very same graduation, one graduate who handed me a rose had been working full-time while going to college. As we sat and visited, she shared, "Michele, I didn't even know what a Dean's List was. When I looked at my grade, I realized I have been on it every semester!" Seeing people fulfill their lifelong dreams and aspirations is inspiring. These kinds of statements fill my bucket to overflowing! It goes to show that people can change and they appreciate the opportunity they are given through Momentum, on their journey to getting there.

BUSINESS AS USUAL

In *Momentum*, we always start with the end in mind and that is engaging individuals in understanding their values. When you correlate values with understanding what it takes to change, as well as transitioning through the stages of change, there is harmony. It is vital to align work and personal values.

I have heard many businesspeople say recently, "People just do not want to work these days."

My response is "Not true!" and also, "You are looking in the wrong places or eliminating a population of people who desire sustainable fulfilling employment."

There is a reason for our mission and values to align.

Dean Feltes, my husband of 41 years, is the most insightful man that I have ever met. He has been given the gift of discernment. It could have come from his years of being a church leader. He listened to and had the opportunity to lead families from five African countries under one church, blending nationalities, languages, and ministry styles.

That experience has assisted Dean in being able to proficiently communicate with diverse populations of individuals regardless of race, ethnicity, political affiliation, individual beliefs, and mindsets. The first time several of us told him how well he spoke on diversity, equity, and inclusion, he was in denial. I love him, so of course I am biased and prone to build up and come to his defense. We have been together longer than we have lived life as singles. But when others around us recognized his God-given knowledge and wisdom, he began to see it himself.

A few of Dean's mentees, who were part of the "Young Guns" rising leader group, concluded that he is truly the G.O.A.T.-Greatest Of All Time. His extensive wisdom and encyclopedic knowledge of random facts make him the undisputed GOAT.

One Christmas, I had a friend design a logo of a goat that said- F.O.U.I. (Fountain Of Useful Information) "Why follow the herd?" Anyone who knows Dean has a strong realization he is no quitter and that he challenges the status quo with a strong foundation based on his faith, knowledge, and wisdom.

Dean is not boastful and quite frankly, he is a solid leader who people want to listen to when he speaks. He is humble and loves what he does. Because it comes naturally to him, he does not always realize his superpower.

> We know businesses want to expand and grow but with the employment crisis, it is a challenge to retain and keep staff.

It resonated with him when a friend stated, "You can speak to industry leaders and get their attention because many of the owners of companies are fifty-something or older white men."

Dean responded, "I resemble that remark!"

Dean is dedicated to equity and helping people and companies fulfill their purpose. When we founded One City United's Momentum Urban Employment program, we adapted it to suit our city's needs. Dean recognized it as an opportunity to transform families and businesses. He saw the potential to shift trajectories through Momentum's organic approach.

Momentum teaches previously marginalized people, many of whom lived in generational poverty, to see options to turn what they once saw as their greatest weakness into their own story of transformation and newfound strength.

We know businesses want to expand and grow but with the employment crisis, it is a challenge to retain and keep staff. Dean told me, "I believe the millennials have it right. They want more and know what they want. They will not settle for less."

This means we are beyond the days of "Just get a job." This is why we advise organizational leaders to better understand the needs of their company, help existing employees to grow professionally, and advance and hire according to values. That's a good start.

Our research shows that companies must evolve, or they cannot compete in today's market. I recently researched the top employee retention benefits for 2023, as identified by some of the country's leading employment advisors.

Research from some of the top employment companies include: ADP, Slack, Forbes, Work Human, indeed, Bamboo HR, and Ramsey Solutions *Citations on final page.

I am sharing my research on what the above leading business advisors and employment experts have indicated are what is important to retain top talent and what they rate as the reason people leave employment.

These are a few thoughts on retention to consider:

At One City United we begin with aligning values. In Business Leadership Today readers are advised to rate values high,

"Define Values in Tangible, Observable, Measurable, and Coachable Terms. Too many leaders assume that every player knows what their core values mean. Unfortunately, many values, no matter how simple, are often left to interpretation. For example, many of our clients list "integrity" as one of their values. At one such client, we asked twenty leaders to define "integrity," specifically as it applies to their organization. We received 19 different answers. If twenty leaders couldn't provide a specific definition, how can those leaders (and those who work for them) be expected to demonstrate that value in daily interactions? *(Bamboo HR)*

This is why a company's values must be defined in tangible, observable, measurable, and coachable terms. Keep it simple! For instance, a behavior that would show alignment to the integrity value might be: "I do what I say I will do." *(Skipper et al.)*

Close pay gaps. Use the data available to you from HR to identify areas of pay disparity (between roles, within departments, etc.) and close those gaps. This can also have a knock-on effect on an employee's bonuses, benefits, and perks. *(Bamboo HR)*

Pay them what they are worth. *(Ramsey Solutions)*

Standardize your compensation strategy. Data is your friend. Comparing your compensation offerings with other businesses means you can remain informed and competitive in the marketplace.

Professional development was rated 4th, "Businesses that offer their employees growth paths and professional development opportunities — including upskilling when required — can increase employee retention and satisfaction."(ADP)

According to an online resource, slack blogger wrote, "Another big reason employees leave a job is a lack of career advancement opportunities. Says Mulligan, "Clearly, career growth needs to happen more quickly, when 68% of organizations are experiencing their highest turnover sometime within a new employee's first 12 months on the job." *(Slack)*

> Sometimes just sharing the rationale behind your pay decisions is one of the best employee retention ideas you can implement.

Be transparent. Honesty and transparency go a long way. Sometimes just sharing the rationale behind your pay decisions is one of the best employee retention ideas you can implement. A SHRM survey found that 91% of employees who believe their company is transparent about pay decisions are also more likely to trust their organization to pay people equally regardless of gender, race, and ethnicity. Not only do these open conversations make your employees feel more valued and fairly compensated, but they also help to create a stronger company culture. *(Bamboo HR)*

Work Human rates Recognition as one of the things many companies with high employee retention rates have in common is their use of employee recognition. (Work Human) Founder, Eric Mosley shared the three elements being purpose, meaning, and gratitude in all playing significant roles in employment today. *(Brown and Mosley)*

Forbes also rated recognition high, #5. Recognize and Reward Your Employees for Their Work. Employees who feel appropriately recognized and rewarded by workplaces are much easier to retain long term, but studies also show those employees will work harder and be more productive. Unfortunately, over 80% of American employees say they don't feel recognized or rewarded.

A report by the Brandon Hall Group found companies that prioritize recognizing their employees multiple times per month are 41% more likely to see increased employee retention and 34% more likely to see increased employee engagement." *(Forbes)*

SHRM = Society for Human Resource Management

I am not sure when recognition faded in the workplace. What I commonly see happen within our classroom are individuals coming into class with a "What's in it for me?" attitude. By the time they graduate a fellowship has been built. The analogy or comparison I use is it's like everyone's taking a selfie on their phone. By the end of the six weeks, they all care for one another so much that it is a big group photo, and nobody can be left out of the picture. Accountability for one another and their success in completion becomes a priority. The point is recognition can be shared, and peer recognition is as important as that given by supervisors and management.

Do the best you can until you know better.
Then when you know better, do better.

~ Maya Angelou

CHAPTER TWO
Solving the Problem Created
Our New Hustle

OUR NEW HUSTLE: A REAL-LIFE REVOLUTION

We had to change our hustle and see life differently.

In 2000, my husband and I uprooted our young family to move from the country to the mid-sized town of Independence, Iowa. When I say young family; our oldest son was a high school senior, our daughter was not yet in middle school, and our youngest son was not yet in school.

The city of Independence's motto is "America's Fame is in Our Name." While there, we explored various careers: Dean went into insurance, working for both captive and independent agencies. He left that industry to work for the Pepsi Corporation, then he became a Pastor in Waterloo, Iowa.

I worked for Dean in insurance, very briefly, and vowed "That will never happen again!"

Afterward, I began a healthcare career, which led to consulting.

We were both raised on farms: Dean, a hog farm, and me, a dairy farm. We virtually had no diversity in our rural, white, roots.

I clearly remember the day Dean told me he was being called into the ministry. However, four years prior, when he left his employment as a general manager for an independent insurance agency; I reacted to the news in a harsh, belittling way. I gave him a snide comment "What are you going to do? Be a *pastor?!?*" Back then, I had a champagne taste on a beer budget. We were living in our dream home, in one of the highest-taxed neighborhoods in Iowa.

Several years later, the day came when Dean shared that he *was* called to be a pastor. God did a miracle in me, but it had taken some years. I said with certainty, "It's about time you figured that out!" Like I knew it all along. "I knew it all along!" I exclaimed. The funny thing was, both our families responded that same way. Four years later I was a pastor's wife who was starting to understand my purpose. Which was looking for change where it's needed and influencing others to see themselves with talents, skills, passion, and purpose. In Christian terms, seeing a city and individuals as God wants me to see them and help others understand that we all can change. Romans 12 became our life chapter and the work we aspired to do.

Dean had taken a position with Pepsi delivering products on a rural route. He worked crazy, early morning hours. He left the house at 3 am and returned home around 3 pm to spend the afternoons with our children. Then he'd leave for Waterloo (30 minutes away), to serve as a supply pastor at a small Wesleyan Church in the Maywood neighborhood of Waterloo, Iowa. Our oldest son received stability even though he had been uprooted his senior year of high school. Both our daughter and youngest son needed that precious time they spent with him.

 The downer was that I was paid to look for what was wrong. I would find it, create a report on it with corrective measures.

At the same time, I started a career in healthcare advancing quickly. I started as an activity coordinator and advanced to being a marketing director for a local long-term care facility. I changed companies, advancing into consulting where I traveled statewide. The downer was that I was paid to look for what was wrong. I would find it and, create a report on it with corrective measures.

Whenever I found a serious compliance issue my boss would say "That means job security!" Like it or not. I really did Not! I am wired to look for the best which I now do daily. My core values were not in sync.

If you have not lost a job, you haven't lived. I was forced to make an ethical decision and lost the consulting position. I remember being at our very small struggling church in the Maywood neighborhood, lying on the floor in the sanctuary reading a book about *The Toxic Workplace. (Chapman and White)*

It hit me, I was given a gift! I had been in the stages of grief after losing my big-wig position, answering to two or three bigger wigs, depending on the day. The realization came to me that day. In ministry, we were seeking what God was calling us to do in Waterloo. I needed to hand the plan over to God fully.

We ran very hard in those early days in ministry, literally. Back and forth from Independence to Waterloo and vice versa. We read Shane Claiborne's book, *The Irresistible Revolution,* after our daughter Jordan went on a mission trip to Africa. We were both learning our shadow mission. It involved kids from the worst, dilapidated, trailer park in the city; the homeless, the addicted, and a huge vision for change. It became our real-life revolution.

It was fitting that our church was called *Realife.* When combining Real-life with revolution, it meant a complete and radical change for us. And that is what happened. Our prayer was "God send us the people you want us to love." I don't know if you pray powerful prayers like this, but when you do, be ready! God answered our prayers and continues to do so today. Some real hurting and struggling people started attending our church. In particular, we began encountering individuals experiencing homelessness.

In 2010, we were living comfortably and foreseeing that within years we would be empty-nesters in our home in the affluent Terrace Drive neighborhood. Well, that vision changed quickly when we found ourselves sharing our living space with nine hurting individuals who needed a hand up.

It all started when we took in an elderly grandmother and her school-aged granddaughter. I was a Big Sister, in the Big Brother Big Sister organization, to her middle school granddaughter who she raised. Grandma needed multiple surgeries.

Then, a teenage boy, who had been sleeping on a park bench in Lafayette Park in Waterloo, was brought to a church service. He moved in with us. He also brought his newly-wedded father and his bride, who also moved in.

We also made room for an older woman who was experiencing homelessness and staying during the day in the Hospitality House. It's a day shelter. She taught me a lot about mental health and the need for community-based housing. Several twenty-somethings called our place home as well. One was a homeless musician and his girlfriend, and another was a young man who was seeking to understand his own purpose.

Is this all getting a little weird for you yet?

During this time, I felt we needed a life skills program within the house. I had researched what they were doing in other parts of the country, and prayed we could implement one. This prayer was later answered in 2018.

One night as Dean and I were watching the nightly news in our spacious living room; the newlyweds walked in from a summer's walk downtown. The husband, Evan, gave me a very proud smile as they walked in the entry. He is one of the sweetest individuals we know. He also makes the strongest coffee I've ever had in my life!

Evan said, "Michele, we got something for you!" They were both beaming from ear to ear. We could not see the surprise they were holding as there was a built-in TV cabinet dividing our foyer.

When he held up the gift, you might imagine OUR surprise when we saw a beautiful red geranium, roots, dirt, and all! He proudly stated, "We got this for you downtown!" While they were still smiling brightly, you can imagine our dismay.

With a knot in my throat, and barely able to speak due to shock and surprise, I responded, "Oh in a planter box downtown?" Gasp! I wanted to crawl into a hole.

ALL LIVES CAN CHANGE!

#WCL

My mind started racing as my subconscious reminded me of all the reasons why this was NOT okay. Especially living in an affluent neighborhood, where people are watching. But then I reminded myself that we are doing life radically different - God's way. So, I needed to wake up and smell the geraniums or at least investigate this matter further.

With a little more probing, I learned it came out of the planter box in front of our neighbor Gary's law firm. I looked at Dean, nearly ready to fall out of my chair laughing, yet trying to hold my composure so I did not embarrass them, and said, "So you want to be in ministry?" Laughing between us, yet holding our composure, we turned back to address the thoughtfulness of the couple.

The couple truly did not grasp that taking that geranium was wrong. They just wanted to make me happy. This law-abiding citizen cleared it with Gary, after a good laugh and he understood there was no ill intent. The twenty-somethings went with me the following evening to replant the geranium - roots and all! Ironically, Gary's law firm ended up doing some pro bono work for Evan's son. Aren't some people just awesome?

PIG MAN

Evan is a very hard-working individual. He ended up taking the first job he could find. This was probably the life lesson I needed to best understand people's values should match their work.

I love success stories. Evan's is one of my favorites. Evan quit that job holding a broom and waiting to sweep up sawdust at the local cabinet manufacturer, after his first day. Because standing and holding a broom while waiting to sweep up the mess, did not correlate with his work values. Interestingly, Evan was not alone in his reasoning. He was not afraid to stand for what he truly desired (aka not afraid to 'quit').

 The next week, we jokingly dubbed Evan "Pigman" because within days he interviewed with a large hog farmer.

So many folks at our church were frustrated he quit a "good-paying job." He had a background of addiction, and they were thrilled he got that job in the first place because the job market was not easy in those days. I was watching and wondering.

The next week, we jokingly dubbed Evan "Pigman" because within days he interviewed with a large hog farmer. Who would have thought? This man, rough around the edges, had a huge passion for caring for farm animals, especially swine.

I remember him coming home and telling me about a worker abusing a pig and he had to stop him. Next thing, I knew he was being promoted. It has been a joy seeing Evan live in his passion and purpose.

Like many people in his position, Evan had a tough upbringing. His mother left him with his father when he was 3 years old. She returned when he was sixteen and he accepted her apology. Evan has been sober for more than 18 years. He moved up in the farming industry, relocating, and purchasing a truck and house. Today, he is financially stable, and he is a loving father and grandfather.

I continue to be amazed at how this process works. When people are filled with hope and transformational opportunities, and choose to embrace forgiveness, their lives start to change. Our mantra way back then became hope, change, and opportunity.

RESEARCH

As we continued our new "housing" service, we researched what organizations in other states and cities were doing. We had been conducting this anecdotal research for years. I researched issues related to poverty, the lack of youth programming, and the impact of gangs as a result of my personal experiences. I lost kids in my youth programs to, you guessed it . . . gangs.

What I discovered was that the reason kids became gang members was due to boredom, economics, and a sense of belonging. The common denominator was incarcerated fathers, and I wanted to understand more.

> What I discovered was that the reason kids became gang members was due to boredom, economics, and a sense of belonging.

Our city, Waterloo, has become a hub for incarceration and returning citizens. Every year over 800 individuals return home, to our city, from prison and/or jail. It's common to hear people from other parts of the state in the Department of Corrections comment, "What is going on in Waterloo?" This is usually followed by emphasizing the number of convictions and violations performed by individuals returning to prison, from Waterloo.

The need for change stems from the daily gaps we witness that hinder people's ability to successfully reintegrate into society. People come here from state and federal prisons as well as the county jail to restart their lives. The dilemma is how?

They are placed on supervision which means probation and/or parole. Some people are directly released and decide to remain in our city.

> Incarceration does not just impact the individual but rather the entire family unit.

There is a common joke amongst justice-impacted individuals when they meet a new person who is visiting our city: "Come to Waterloo on vacation and stay on probation."

Incarceration does not just impact the individual but rather the entire family unit. The children I interacted with had family members who were incarcerated. I spent months interviewing many returned citizens and had to look at all aspects of incarceration.

We were working in ministry in the most impoverished areas of Waterloo. Every week, we encountered marginalized individuals facing substantial barriers to employment. These people needed services but also expressed frustration with their circumstances. It took a lot of faith and fortitude to find the right avenues to assist people because we had no lived experience. I guess this is what they mean about God equipping the ill equipped. Trusting people can be difficult for individuals who've been impacted by the justice system.

 We were convinced there must be a program that could equip these individuals with the skills needed to overcome the obstacles holding them back. That is when we realized there really wasn't much. We wanted to journey with people. It was hard seeing them suffer and we knew something had to give.

During my pursuit of a master's degree with an emphasis in nonprofit leadership, the most challenging research I undertook was for my social justice paper, which delved into the issues surrounding incarceration in Iowa.

At the time, I was running a six-year privately funded program for children that focused on strengths and abilities. We used the performing arts as the avenue to engage elementary through high school kids. During my research, I found a 24/7 Wall Street Report in 2015 that was very alarming. (Thomas C. Frohlich) It rated Waterloo near the top of the list in being the "Worst Place in America for Black People to Live." My new neighbor was photographed walking in our inner city Waterloo neighborhood, in an online article. That gave me an uneasy feeling and a bit of a reality check to see her portrayed that way. I was shocked that a city as small as ours rated worse than many metropolitan areas. It all seemed to lead back to incarceration. I really needed to know.

COMMUNITY DEVELOPMENT CAN CHANGE EVERYTHING

Fast forward to 2018, when the mayor of Waterloo, Quentin Hart, met with us to discuss the future vision of One City United. Before this, I had introduced Mayor Hart to Tim Diesburg, who previously served as the Supervisor Apprenticeship Coordinator of Iowa Prison Industries (IPI).

My goal was twofold: First, for the mayor to gain a better understanding of apprenticeship programs, and second, for Tim to comprehend the reasons behind the disproportionately high number of Black men from Waterloo being incarcerated in Iowa prisons – a phenomenon he had witnessed firsthand during his tenure as a prison employee.

I wanted Tim to hear about racism in our city from the mayor. I wanted Mayor Hart to share the perspective prevalent in East Waterloo, where Iowa Prison Industries was perceived as a form of "new slave labor."

Mayor Hart shared his perceptions and the perspectives of our community about what he had heard about IPI from Waterloo citizens whose families had been to prison. He learned from Tim that the skills being taught in IPI were transferring into good jobs for those returning home from prison.

During my initial research at the prison, I told Tim, "If we did what you are doing in the prisons but instead out here in the community, paying a good living wage, educating in the earn and learn model – people would not return to prison!" Tim's response was "Do it! You can do it!"

At our meeting, I wanted them to both understand the conflict I was seeing. I will share the conflicts of interest I personally see, related to incarceration, later in this chapter.

To finish this meeting with Mayor Hart and Tim I channeled my inner activist, even though my superpower is more closely rooted in advocacy as a "Recidivism Disruptor." That aligns with my wholehearted desire to not just accept the status quo.

Please understand that I love finding solutions so we can quickly eliminate barriers as they present themselves. However, the process is slower than I prefer.

At a later date, Mayor Hart called to get Tim's contact information from me. He wanted Tim to speak at a breakout session at the Future Ready Iowa Conference in Cedar Falls (an affluent town adjacent to Waterloo) in 2018. I had explained to Mayor Hart, that we have an important reentry meeting scheduled at the very time he wanted Tim to speak at the conference.

Mayor Hart made a call to one of the Iowa Works coordinators who oversaw the event and learned the event was sold out. He said, "It's sold out! But you can walk in with Tim!" We did. Many of our board members were in attendance. When we heard the keynote speakers present, all the One City Board Members in attendance started smiling and looking at one another. I believe we were all thinking the same thing - THIS IS THE SKILLS PROGRAM WE HAVE BEEN LOOKING FOR!

A couple of things happened that day at the *2018 Future Ready Iowa* Conference that would start to transform and unify the city of Waterloo.

1) The news broke at the conference that Waterloo/Cedar Falls, Iowa ranked #1 for the Worst City for Blacks to Live on the *24/7 Wall Street Report. (Samuel Stebbins)*

2) Tim and I followed the speakers out the door which led to the launching of One City's Momentum Urban Employment Initiative, meeting our mission of Filling Gaps & Equipping People.

THE CONFLICTS OF INTEREST I SEE

For lawmakers to consider: Occasionally legislators do not fully understand the impact of their decisions. It is crucial to inform decision-makers about the potential ramifications of their actions so they can fully understand the consequences. I am going to list some things I see as quandaries that should be addressed by our lawmakers.

These decisions have inadvertently done more harm than help. Oh, here I am being a disruptor again.

The conflicts I found in my research were:

1) Teaching skills versus the fact that state entities must buy from Iowa Prison Industries.

Problem: They've built their own client base which increases the need to incarcerate human beings. Lawmakers can change who oversees the apprenticeship programs. However, it does not eliminate the problem of **needing** to incarcerate people. Two words that concern me are: supply and demand.

2) Skills versus many being paid cents on the dollar.

Problem: This prevents inmates from sending money home to provide for their own families and/or accumulating a nest egg for when they successfully return home. Former inmates receive $100 as they leave prison.

3) State legislation withholding driver's licenses due to offenses that are unrelated to driving. Unfortunately, transportation is a problem in many cities. The Cedar Valley continues to look for solutions.

Problem: In Waterloo, Iowa we have no public transportation after 6pm and our routes do not run to the industries. How do these legislative and policy decisions affect and impact our job market and our economy? These practices negatively impact the workforce and not only individuals but entire families . . . Possibly for generations.

I digress . . .

One City United's solution: We started a transportation shuttle service called TO WORK, "We drive people to employ people." In our Momentum classes, we teach networking so well that very few of our graduates have needed to utilize this much needed service. It ran nearly 24/7 with a coordinator and round-the-clock drivers. We celebrated when someone would get their driver's license and save enough money for a vehicle. That is what we do and who we are at One City! Drivers were also great encouragers when someone had a hard time at work. It was common to see drivers swing by to access the clothing closet because a rider just returned to the men's or women's work facility from jail or prison. As of December 2024, this three-year program came to an end. Many private companies have emerged. We celebrate their entrepreneurial spirit! One City now looks to the next gap to fill.

I remember the night I met civil rights legend Representative John Lewis "the conscience of Congress," as he walked through our local Kwik Star convenience store, with his aide. Based on an online article I read, he was likely at the store to buy bananas and water for the caucus event taking place that evening.

After researching incarceration rates in Iowa, I was deeply discouraged by my findings. When welcoming Rep. John Lewis to the city, I greeted him along these lines: "Welcome to Waterloo, Senator Lewis. Welcome to a city that has a higher per capita rate of disproportionate incarceration for Black men than any other city in the nation."

I was so very nervous I pronounced the word *disproportionately* wrong, and he kindly corrected me. I know that was no way to welcome an esteemed Senator, but I just knew he was here in Waterloo to make a call for change! He was here to campaign for Hillary Clinton. I wanted Rep. Lewis to know that this white church lady saw the conflict in what I was seeing, and I was not okay with it. I digress...

THROUGH THE EYES OF A CHILD

Our initial focus was on addressing barriers faced by children, which led to witnessing how families were impacted by the stigma associated with unemployment. For six years, we worked with kids through a program called ATEV (Arts To End Violence), which we developed in response to the violence plaguing our community.

This became the training ground for us on tenacity. We had started this work with high school youth from our church. This white church lady fell in love with the beauty of diversity, equity, and inclusion. "White Church Lady" was the name the kids' families called me when I'd pull up in the church van. That is until they got to know and trust me as just "Michele." This program taught us so much about the challenges that families were facing:

- **Single moms** who did not have gas money to drive their kids to the program.
- **Lack of funds** for food, clothing, and extras that we all take for granted.
- **Incarcerated** fathers.

- **Homelessness** Families facing eviction and experiencing homelessness would have to live in a hotel for temporary shelter.
- Oh and let's not forget about **the violence** breaking out in all their neighborhoods.

Our program prevented kids from being on "lockdown." This is something that parents do to protect their children in violent riddled neighborhoods.

One middle schooler wrote a lament song that shared his pain when his mother was hit by gunfire after their house was pelted with 17 rounds.

ATEV became a place where the world seemed to be much smaller because of the beauty of diversity. It became a place where there was no judgment. We had immigrant children from several African countries, as well as children from Mexico.

All these barriers related to the parents' lack of sustainable, fulfilling employment: childcare, transportation, housing/homelessness, criminal background, addictions/in recovery, ageism, generational poverty, and unemployment.

Even though ATEV was predominantly Black/African American, we had no color lines. The kids all got to know each other's cultures. We incorporated diverse perspectives into the programming. We used the performing arts (hip hop and dance) to bring kids together, instill kids with a sense of belonging, and keep them safe from the streets.

One of the most treasured gifts I have ever received was a bumper sticker that one of the boys gave me that said "Justice for Donnisha" because his sister had been murdered. That was a Holy gift. He gave that bumper sticker as a selfless gift, sharing his family's tragedy so I could see and understand his pain.

In our work with the children, we realized the needs of the parents were not being met. All these barriers related to the parents' lack of sustainable, fulfilling employment: childcare, transportation, housing/homelessness, criminal background, addictions/in recovery, ageism, generational poverty, and unemployment.

One City tabled the ATEV program, which the kids renamed Arts to Enrich Values, before launching *Momentum Urban Employment in Waterloo*. Ironically, it was a month before the pandemic made it to America, that we halted the ATEV program. We have had three parents of kids come through and graduate Momentum. This has ultimately changed the trajectory of their families. Regardless of the barrier we have witnessed lives being transformed by some tenacious people who desire change for themselves and their families!

Find a job you enjoy doing and you will never have to work a day in your life.

~ Mark Twain

CHAPTER THREE
Just the Why?
Steps, Structure & Organization

The pandemic of 2020 introduced The Great Resignation.

If you are reading this book, you are likely seeking to comprehend the driving forces behind the "Great Resignation" phenomenon and the reasons for the disproportionately high employee turnover rates your company is experiencing compared to other organizations.

Why is this happening?

Employers need a paradigm shift in their HR Hiring policies and practices.

FIX THE DAMN ROOF

As we established the non-profit One City United, we researched initiatives undertaken by other cities to alleviate poverty and how community development played a crucial role in those efforts.

A decade ago, in his TEDx talk "Fix the Damn Roof!," Johnny Turnipseed shared how 10 of his family members were convicted of first-degree murder due to the absence of a father figure. He powerfully stated, "The roof in a child's life is his father. The father protects them." After turning his own life around through faith and mentorship, Turnipseed dedicated his remaining years to helping wayward or absentee fathers fix themselves and their families. It was at Urban Ventures in South Minneapolis where Johnny Turnipseed, who had radically transformed his life, implored us, "Fix the damn roof!"

One man, Art Erickson, Urban Ventures Founder, believed in him. Together they took on economic disparities in South Minneapolis. Johnny was passionate about getting to the problems and root causes in each person's life. Turnipseed's "Fix the Damn Roof" analogy highlighted how the following can produce profound life changes:

- Excellent education that
- Promotes transformational thinking
- Combined with mentoring
- By culturally and socially competent individuals.

This analogy helped people understand the power of such an approach.

"Fix the Damn Roof." YouTube, YouTube, www.youtube.com/results?search_query=Fix%2Bthe%2BDamn%2BRoof%2BTed%2BTalk. Accessed 26 Aug. 2024.

Johnny gave us a way to explain to people that we need to work together to be solution based. Once we get to the root cause, we can work to address it and end the problem. Then we can all move onto the next problem. Collaborative work is the answer. While valuable work was being done in Waterloo, we saw a pressing need for organizations to collaborate and shift their focus away from competing for program funding. Instead, they needed to collectively prioritize addressing the critical needs present within our community.

We brought together people of good work and people of faith to make these changes. Art and Johnny were passionate about this! Johnny's story of childhood trauma and the radical change he made was told in a trilogy of movies called Turnipseed.

Check it out here: "Turnipseed Trilogy." YouTube, youtu.be/KmDU6qILxPc?si=jM-G5ReN6PsJJJRC. Accessed 26 Aug. 2024.

Art connected us to Lee Rainey who had grown up in Waterloo, but spent his professional career in Minneapolis. His parents lived down the street from our church. He was on their board and was instrumental in launching Urban Ventures. He invested in our lives so we could address the holes (gaps) in our roof (our city) that needed to be fixed (by services that provide solutions to the problems). Lee later became my mentor, we met weekly, via phone, for months.

These three wise men, Art, Johnny, and Lee helped us realize we weren't crazy for believing the way we did. They also let us know that we were considered "street practitioners."

Lee gave me the courage to face my fears about advancing my education to better understand poverty in the city we now call home.

I struggled to comprehend the racial disparities, but my new Black and Brown friends extended me a lot of grace, patience, and understanding as I worked on educating myself. Actually, they were educating me and changing the learned biases and preconceived notions that I had.

As I began to understand my own biases, I realized that I said a lot of dumb things that could have been offensive, but I was given the gift of Grace. Maybe because they saw this crazy white church lady who was seeking understanding and solutions.

At times, it seemed like the sociological issues were so deep-seated. I started to understand my own and others' implicit bias. I was a White woman working with Black and Brown kids.

It seemed that altering long-established practices and norms was viewed as an insurmountable challenge. I was crossing some kind of line. Was it a racial line? Maybe.

Black church leaders started attending services to see why Black kids were coming to our church. Was it some kind of a church line? Maybe.

We were doing church differently from any other churches in our denomination. We were filling the church chairs with kids. This was not normal, but it was becoming our normal.

I saw families living in poverty with no path out. I saw a line between the "haves" and the "have-nots." The haves wanted to leave the neighborhoods of the have-nots. It appeared to me that they did not want to stay where it reminded them of a time when they had little.

We needed and continue to need people to reinvest. This is what I saw happening in our city, and I came to find out these same things were happening in other cities as well.

 We were filling the church chairs with kids. This was not normal, but it was becoming our normal.

On the other hand, for those experiencing and living in poverty, it felt like I was watching people implode. It reminded me of the analogy of putting a frog in a pan of water and turning on the fire, slowly raising the heat to the point of boiling.

Not realizing what was happening, the frog doesn't jump out. Poverty and all the secondary economies that are illegal, under cover industries, that become normalized. Secondary economies can be things like fronts for stolen merchandise that are shipped from one town to another, the drug industry, sex trafficking, and the strip club industry. become normalized. I felt like we were in the midst of the boiling water.

> Rather than collaborating to address poverty-related issues together, these organizations seemed to fiercely defend their respective domains, prioritizing the protection of their individual silos.

When we met Johnny Turnipseed, he said to us "There are more than enough nonprofits in Waterloo that just want to keep the problem going so they can continue to exist."

Both Dean and I began to notice that in our community. We called them silos of support, and they were not collaborating. Rather than collaborating to address poverty-related issues together, these organizations seemed to fiercely defend their respective domains, prioritizing the protection of their individual silos. That seemed counterproductive to us. We wondered why they just didn't work together to remove the problems. If they worked to remove a problem, then everyone could move to the next problem. We started to take that viewpoint of developing services that would fix the roof.

When I brought the ATEV (Arts To End Violence) kids to an event at the Waterloo Writing Project, I had the opportunity to share about One City United with the brilliant local historian, Charles Pearson. He posed a thoughtful question to me, "So the group you work with is called Arts to End Violence?"

I answered proudly, "Yes, it is!" Charles responded, "So there has to be violence in our community in order for your group to exist?"

Wow, that hit me like a ton of bricks! Oh my goodness, I was part of the problem! I had enough issues with being the White Church Lady, building trust as a White woman working with a majority of Black and Brown kids, and working on overdrive not to come off as if I had some "White savior complex." Now this? I later posed that very question to the kids and shared what Charles had said. The kids responded with something to the effect of, "I was thinking we are more than about ending violence." They rebranded themselves using the very same acronym A.T.E.V. and became Arts to Enrich Values.

We also learned, from our years of research, that we needed to really understand the community. This was when we started researching other non-profits, local and nationwide.

We went to Urban Ventures in South Minneapolis. Locally, we got involved in activities such as the People's Big Tent Event to do this. People's Health Clinic in East Waterloo serves many individuals on state assistance. We set up a booth there for an annual summer event in 2017 and polled the people (patients and non-profit leaders).

Our founding board member, Lynn Neill, had previously worked worked at People's Health Clinic. Lynn got a spot for One City, with all the other service providers. The ATEV kids performed as part of the entertainment.

Lynn helped me to develop a survey for the attendees that identified gaps, needs, and desires. Transportation and housing were big issues for those patients. However, we also learned that people wanted education and skills but had no path to achieve these goals. Surprisingly, when we surveyed service providers, they did not identify advancing education and skills as a primary concern for their clients.

This was a real Ahh-Haa moment for me. It taught me we should always "Ask the people" and "know our community" before we start making decisions.

Do they need a well for water or do they need a soccer field?

I want to give credit where credit is due and that is with my husband, Dean. He is one of the wisest men I know. He often shares this story about the importance of asking people what they want and need before moving into action:

DEAN'S SOCCER FIELD STORY

About twenty years ago, I was talking with a missionary who was part of a group drilling wells in Africa. People were becoming sick and suffering from disease, many were dying as they drank contaminated water. Their whole mission was to drill wells so people in remote places could have clean drinking water, a fantastic mission.

In one particular community, they were struggling to get buy-in from the local leaders. One "crazy" missionary said, "Let's have a meeting to find out why they are fighting us on drilling this well." So, they sat down with the community leaders and began asking questions. They were told, "We don't want a well, we want a soccer field!" The missionary group was astounded *at this request* because people were continuously becoming sick and many were dying because of the lack of clean water. One wise missionary pressed the issue as to why they wanted a soccer field instead of a well. Their answer was probably profound to most, but makes perfect sense as we come to understand humans and what really makes us tick.

They explained that the two villages closest to them both had soccer fields, and they didn't, so they needed a soccer field. The missionary group got together and discussed how they could get the resources together to build a soccer field. Within a few months, they were building a soccer field with the help of many people in the community. When the project was completed, they held a huge celebration and played soccer on their own field for the first time.

The community leaders wasted no time in asking the group of missionaries if they could help them drill a well now that they had a soccer field. The well was drilled with the help of many people in the community, which provided the entire community with fresh water.

The requests didn't end there. Their next request focused on better farming practices for both crops and livestock. They were connected with a traveling group who came in to do training and work alongside the people in the community.

This ended up being one of the most successful missionary projects they had ever been a part of.

The question is why?

The villagers suffered from low self-esteem, believing they were less valued than neighboring villages - a mindset that affected both how they saw themselves and how they lived their daily lives.

When someone actually listened to them, partnered with them, and brought needed resources into play, hope showed up. As they began to see who they really were, as they began to join in the work of transforming their lives and their community, the world of opportunity opened up to them.

All they needed was for someone to partner with them and journey with them as they began to self-actualize and dream again.

The soccer field made them feel legitimate among their neighbors; the well made them a healthier community, better agriculture made them more prosperous and impacted their health as well. You really don't know what someone needs or even where to start if you don't ask. Transforming a life, transforming a neighborhood, transforming a company or a city... it is a journey that always begins with questions to identify needs. Not the needs that I believe are present, the needs that are real in a person's life at that time.

You may wonder why, in a book focused on employment, employee retention, and transforming company practices and hiring policies, I am sharing stories about a program for kids. It's simple, it all relates to what it goes back to . . . values.

The worldwide pandemic altered almost everyone's world, didn't it? Maybe if you are naturally a hermit or live in very remote areas it didn't change much. For most of us, it changed everything! It is important to understand that we, as a society, allow ourselves to get caught up in the "busyness" of life. We lost sight of our values.

Why did we begin the One City Momentum Urban Employment Initiative during the heat of the pandemic, when everyone else was shutting down? Waterloo was the hot spot for COVID-19 as we started programming.

Because all those needs and gaps, were becoming more like an enormous chasm, not just a gap. For those living in poverty, the gaps increased and magnified. It has become common to hear business owners, corporate leaders, and human resource professionals say, "People just do not want to work!" I'm here to say you are wrong. I will follow up by inquiring:

1) Are you eliminating individuals because you need to remove the stigmas of mental health, recovery, and reentry from your hiring practices?

- How are you personally changing your worldview and viewpoint of what is locally happening around you?
- Has the neighborhood where your business is located changed due to the economic climate?
- How has your company invested in diversity, equity, and inclusion within your organization? Are you happy with the status quo?
- Does your current workforce need to change their perspectives, perceptions, and prejudices?

- If your current employees knew that someone had been hospitalized for mental health reasons, was receiving treatment for addiction, or had previously been incarcerated, would they treat that person differently?
- Does your company need to make a paradigm shift in your policies and practices related to your socio-economic viewpoint?
- Do your company's policies and practices lead to inadvertent decision-making based on perceived societal status? In other words, are decisions being influenced by preconceptions about an individual's socioeconomic status, cultural background, language differences, hairstyles, or even personal hygiene?
- Has your company embraced understanding differences? Are you supporting people with various backgrounds and cultures in your workforce?
- Does your company assist individuals in feeling supported and work with them to find common ground between staff versus the evident differences?

What I'm discussing goes far beyond simply establishing diversity, equity, and inclusion policies within an organization.

The focus is on your company's or organization's willingness to engage in self-reflection and implement changes that prioritize creating a "People-First Culture and Rehumanize Employment." It's about fostering an environment that genuinely puts people at the forefront.

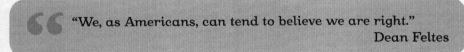

"We, as Americans, can tend to believe we are right."
Dean Feltes

If the information above has prompted self-reflection and led you to consider whether your business practices need reviewing, I encourage you to take the time to read the two poems listed below that profoundly impacted my perspective.

"We, as Americans, can tend to believe we are right." Dean Feltes

That statement is made with a broad brush and can be defined by the word ethnocentrism. If you disagree, at least consider how we differ from so many other countries because we are such an individualistic society. During my time studying Sociology at Hawkeye Community College, I encountered a thought-provoking poem titled "The Body Ritual Among the Nacirema." Written in 1956 by the American anthropologist Horace Miner, this piece offered a unique perspective. I highly recommend taking a look at it.

The second poem is by Julia Dinsmore. She has been an advocate for change and alleviating poverty in Minnesota for many years. We met her at a Christian Community Development Conference (CCDA), in Minnesota. The poem is "My Name Is Not Those People." I purchased the poem. It now hangs in my office at One City United.

MOMENTUM GRADUATES SHARE THEIR SUCCESS STORIES

It has become commonplace for Momentum graduates to stop by and encourage the new classes. It is because they know there is power in the struggle, but they also know the power of peer encouragement.

"This was what I wanted the most! I wanted something different! When I graduated, I got this email for this job at Allen and it needs to be done today - it was me explaining my record, I was nervous and they stayed calm. Michele wrote me a letter of recommendation and with everything she said about me, I got my dream job right here! I never thought I would work in a hospital with a record, but I am and they love me there. Let go and move forward, you can't go wrong!" – **J.K.**

"You have got to be willing to talk about your past, but don't beat yourself up about your past. Your past is your past- leave it there. Just show what you have done since then! I learned that some of my weaknesses can be strengths. Growing up I believed I wasn't supposed to fail. I beat myself up when I failed until I was dead and blue. I had to learn to stop doing that. I had to learn to stop second-guessing myself because I do that a lot. Just believe in yourself and you can do it! Turning Weaknesses into Strengths: My pride was one of my weaknesses, so I turned that into my strength by being prideful. I completed the drug court program because not too many people do - do that! Being able to say ' You know what, I have been clean and sober for almost two years! Sometimes being outgoing can be a weakness but I can turn that into a leadership skill. I can utilize that leadership (outgoingness) as a leadership skill because I can say ' You know what when I become a team lead my goal is- at the beginning of our shift, when we get our carts ready, have a little pow wow saying 'This is what we are going to do tonight, we are going to do this, we are going to get this done and we are gonna go home and be happy with what we did!" – **J.H.**

The PROCESS

Understanding change involves being intimately familiar with your company's mission and developing a plan to integrate people in a way that creates opportunities for all. It's about recognizing the intersection where individuals seeking hope, change, and opportunity can positively impact your company, propelling it forward on a new transformative journey.

UNDERSTANDING THE PROBLEMS

Early on we started sharing our research with Community Bank & Trust. I know our bankers probably wondered where this crazy couple came from. Our research on the gaps and stats we were seeing in this city we call home, Waterloo, was significant!

The barriers to overcome and stigmas people faced, such as mental health, recovery, and reentry, all related to unemployment. It sometimes seems that there is a circular motion in poverty. What I mean is one barrier leads to another and people just give up when it gets to be too much.

I spent six hours and three trips to the Department of Transportation with a Momentum graduate who lived here for years, after moving from Chicago. The challenge was that she did not have stable housing and, therefore, no permanent address. Without a permanent address, you cannot get a state ID. Without a state ID, you cannot get employment.

When numbers get entered incorrectly by another agency you must track that down. The Department of Corrections in Illinois entered her number wrong, so it did not match. I had to strongly advocate for this woman. I was so frustrated with the minutiae of this social service nightmare! I am not surprised that some people just give up and stay in a system that sets people up to fail.

Iowa needs paid advocates and peer support specialists who can guide and support individuals as they navigate their way out of systems that perpetuate poverty.

If you ever have the opportunity to participate in a poverty and/or incarceration simulation, do it!

REHUMANIZING EMPLOYMENT IN A PEOPLE-FIRST CULTURE TAKES GRIT

When Dean and I began *One City's Momentum* I worked as a Job Developer and Job Coach for a non-profit serving individuals with disabilities in the workforce. One City facilitated a collaboration with my employer and one of the largest employers in the Cedar Valley and Iowa.

We asked the employer's operations manager about their hiring policies and practices. Dean challenges the status quo in a very nonjudgmental, yet direct manner, because when policies do not make sense, profits, and people first culture can suffer. We were both very impressed by the work they do but realized they could do even better if we challenged a silly policy about not hiring someone who had a driving offense within a specified, period of time.. It was a long-standing human resource policy. Dean asked, "Why is that policy in place when the employee is working in the warehouse and would not be driving for their position?" Their team reviewed it, and the policy was changed. *One City* collaborated on our first internship for *Momentum Urban Employment.* Through that one opportunity they hired one of our graduates, Lance. He would not have been hired if the original policies remained in place.

At One City, we work on both ends of employment: the potential employees and the potential employers. This proved to be very advantageous for the employer in Lance's case.

I had convinced Lance to attend Momentum's open enrollment. He was part of my research on issues related to incarceration in Iowa. Lance was not a young man, he was 70 years old at the time and had been frustrated about the denial letters he repeatedly received from companies.

Lance shined brightly in the internship. He loves competition especially when his alma mater, Iowa State plays against the Iowa Hawkeyes. Lance's role has taken him from being an intern to being known as the fastest shipper in the company's fulfillment center division. They have four fulfillment locations nationwide. Lance is fully vested in this Employee Stock Ownership Plan (ESOP), through his workplace, and he continues to love his position to this day.

I believe that this company did not expect that the change they made in their hiring policies and practices would net them such a valued employee. But it did.

Everything that happened played a significant role in advancing the Future Ready Iowa Vision that included One City United.

Consider this . . .

To change company culture leaders need to realize they must to first admit there is a problem with the current culture. I want you, as a reader of this book, a leader in your respected community, and as someone who wants to see your corporation invest in people, to take a step back and pause . . .

Take an hour to consider:

- The people who have been employed but had to leave your company due to policies you have in place.
- The people you cannot hire because of policies in place.
- The waiting period employees must endure before becoming eligible for benefits like health insurance. Reflect on the potential life events or challenges that could arise for an employee during this probationary timeframe, where they must prove themselves before receiving those benefits.
- The complicated website that individuals must navigate to be considered for a position. Consider applying to your own company and see how difficult it is to navigate your company's online application. **If you do that add on another hour because trust me, you might need it!**

I'll see you after an undistracted hour of considering how you have lost good employees or not hired individuals due to their past because of long-standing (even decades old) policies.

Inclusion isn't just inviting someone to sit at your table. It's believing they belong there.

~ Mia Carella

Community Bank & Trust listened to the needs and gaps we were seeing in the cedar valley before One City United became a non-profit. After listening they supported the work of One City's Momentum employment program. Their president, Stacey Bentley, invited Dean to round table discussions with other service providers. We were extremely grateful to see the bank begin to represent the community they serve. CB&T began to create proactive programs that would assist our graduates and other service providers in saving and having emergency funds. These are rightly so-called Community Cares and Safety Net savings accounts. We are forever grateful for their insightful guidance and direction in building Momentum.

Multiple CB&T staff have physically given back by presenting topics on workplace culture, assisted in redesigning interviewing curriculum and participated as mock interviewers. CB&T treats every graduate with respect and dignity. Community Bank & Trust truly invest in community development, equity and opportunity for all.

CHAPTER FOUR

Community Bank & Trust
A President's Perspective

Employing individuals who deserve a second chance fosters an inclusive workplace and taps into a diverse talent pool. This meaningful and intentional action contributes to community as well as community development. As a community banker, this is a viewpoint I strongly support and believe in.

BUT, how did we get there?

To be transparent, this has been and continues to be a journey. There are days, I believe we have made great strides and days I feel we have taken a few steps backward.

I take intentional steps every single day. I was not aware of the importance of hiring individuals who came from diverse backgrounds. It didn't occur to me to be intentional like that. It was not until my firsthand experiences caused me to become aware of the need for diversity. It was at that time that I started to understand the significance of hiring individuals with diverse backgrounds.

I must disclose that this chapter is about my thoughts, views, and perceptions, not necessarily about the bank. I have reviewed and received permission to share this information.

We all need experiences in our lives that help us to learn and grow. Each of us is at a different place in our journey of inclusiveness, and that is ok. Every one of us needs to be willing to take one step further than yesterday. Every. Single. Day. I've grown tremendously through my 40 years of banking.

So, here we are today. I'm happy to say inclusion is a big part of who I represent personally and as a leader at Community Bank and Trust.

Leadership comes with great responsibility. Through visible, meaningful, and intentional action, I hold myself and those around me accountable for creating connections and ensuring a strong sense of welcoming, belonging, and creating a safe space for anyone and everyone who experiences Community Bank and Trust.

> **I'm happy to say inclusion is a big part of who I represent personally and as a leader at Community Bank and Trust.**

It is our culture. Not just today, not just tomorrow, but for the future. It is embedded into the fabric of who we are and not just the words on a page. We are committed to our team members, our clients, and our community. Why? You may be asking why (DEI) diversity, equity, and inclusion is important to us.

Inclusion is important. Everyone deserves to feel included. Let me say that again, EVERYONE deserves to be included. It is not only important to our company because it is "the right thing to do," but also the "smart thing to do."

DEI is also important to our community. When our community is a success, we are all successful. Whether we are citizens, employers, or employees, we all thrive and grow. Our friends and families thrive and grow. We attract new residents, we offer additional services, added events and attractions to gain and retain new residents.

At Community Bank and Trust, we are committed to our strategic DEI initiative and believe that fostering a culture of inclusion is mission-critical for our employees, clients, and communities to not only succeed but thrive!

We work to encourage tough conversations, in a safe place, to learn, grow, and build relationships through trust.

Trust happens when you can have a conversation with no repercussions. This prompts me to share a story about a young woman who has improved our inclusion efforts.

This young woman has helped our bank grow financially by being one of our top referral partners. She has also aided Community Bank and Trust to grow internally by assisting young managers to learn new techniques and management skills in communication.

I met a graduate through a referral from Dean and Michele Feltes. Both Dean and Michele thought this graduate would be a good fit for our bank. Our initial meeting led me to believe this Momentum graduate would be an excellent hire for our bank.

> At Community Bank and Trust, we are committed to our strategic DEI initiative and believe that fostering a culture of inclusion is mission-critical for our employees, clients, and communities to not only succeed but thrive!

This graduate was personable and had an uncanny ability to communicate - it just felt right. Here is the key point: "It's the person, not the background" we should consider. The graduate was honest and said she did not want a banking career long-term, as she had other aspirations. I persuaded her to give this opportunity a try. She needed benefits and a job. We had a community banker position available and were looking for an individual with a warm, cheerful personality along with the ability to communicate with our clients. This graduate had a ready smile and a helpful attitude and went on to become a valuable member of our CBT team.

When this individual started her role as a community banker, there were also two managerial position changes occurring, as those managers transitioned into different roles within the organization. I learned several valuable lessons, with one lesson I need to share with you. It is straightforward, and yet, so simple.

In my reflection, I see where we failed. It was a matter of diverse backgrounds and experiences. Or rather a lack of diverse backgrounds combined with a deficiency in management skills and/or experiences.

You see, our company recently hired a diversity, inclusion, and equity officer. This individual's focus was on leveraging our differences, raising awareness, and providing training to intentionally and consistently further Community Bank and Trust's diversity, equity, and inclusion (DEI) journey through education.

The bank's current manager was open, shared a willingness to learn, and was keenly aware they lacked diverse backgrounds.

Both individuals had grown up in small towns in Iowa, with little to no diversity. The managers simply lacked training or the background to communicate and manage individuals of various origins.

Before this time, the bank provided minimal training. I did not mention this earlier, but the employee we hired is of color and sports tattoos and a nose piercing. The two managers were Caucasian, with no visible tattoos or piercings. These characteristics are basic visible differences and bring to light the diversity among individuals.

Once this employee joined the banking team, communication issues became evident. She felt managers were targeting her or talking beneath her capabilities. The managers were frustrated as well. Most importantly though, the happy, bubbly employee I had hired lost the personality previously noted.

 We are learning and growing, and we strongly believe in the spirit of diversity.

It was apparent issues had arisen. The managers attempted to communicate and open their minds to learning and growing in their inclusion journey. I appreciated the employee for assisting our team members through the concerns and her patience as we acknowledged our deficiencies.

She approached tough conversations with openness and honesty. When a manager asked her how Community Bank and Trust could help address communication barriers, she responded, "Hire more people like me and transition away from the traditional banking employee appearance."

We are learning and growing, and we strongly believe in the spirit of diversity.

It is essential that we not only respect one another's differences but also strategically leverage those differences to our advantage.

At the same time, we must identify common ground and areas of intersectionality to serve as a strong foundation for building a better business.

Everyone has the right to feel a sense of welcome, belonging, and safety when they do business at Community Bank and Trust. We must do this internally and externally, for our employees, clients, and community.

As I mentioned earlier, one step forward every single day. This was the message I shared at our internal employee development event we held in October 2023 on Diversity, Equity, and Inclusion.

We are not perfect, we make mistakes. Yet, I can assure you, we care, and we are trying to be a little bit better every single day. That equates to being a whole lot better over time. Although we host these workshops for our team, we know this journey has to be in the forefront every day.

In today's world, fostering a diverse workforce is a strategic business decision. We want to be known as a Community Bank that makes a difference. Our team lives, works, and raises their families here.

I see companies "write the check." It is easier to "write the check" and see your business name displayed. It looks great on the poster, PowerPoint, and social media posts. But at the end of the day, when the check has cleared, you need to ask yourself . . . what is next?

> We are not perfect, we make mistakes. Yet, I can assure you, we care, and we are trying to be a little bit better every single day.

We believe the behavior and actions must follow the check. At Community Bank and Trust, it is not "either"/or." It is "yes/and."

Contributing money is needed but also volunteering your time and talents are needed as well. Every employee is encouraged to give back. The employees of CBT, 34 in total, have volunteered 1,000+ hours annually to help support Cedar Valley non-profit organizations.

In late 2023, our QCRH holding company granted the 700+ employees 8 hours each of paid time annually to volunteer at their nonprofit of choice.

This leads me to a difficult topic to discuss. It is an important part of who I am today. I have family members who have struggled with addiction and mental illness. I am extremely grateful a few employers took a chance on them, and allowed them to gain employment, regardless of their history.

History does not define us, it shapes us. My favorite word since the pandemic is GRACE. Allow yourself grace and allow others grace as well. We encourage others to delay judgment.

Barriers are everywhere when it comes to employment. Be intentional in how you approach people, listen to their stories, find a little empathy, and most of all, allow grace. I ask that you keep an open mind, be curious, and try and meet someone halfway on THEIR journey, not your journey.

Naturally, we see the world through our lens, and it is easily influenced by firsthand experiences. I am a better person and leader due to my life experiences both personally and professionally.

We have witnessed that engaging diverse individuals has created an inclusive culture and has fueled innovation. It has generated passion and excitement to be your best self. We have learned diverse teams approach challenges from different angles and celebrate successes in unity. It has allowed us to understand and relate to prospects and clients to better serve the needs of our community.

Although people often think of race or gender when they hear the word diversity, diversity goes beyond the things we can see. All employees need to feel valued for their unique contributions, which in turn leads to improved retention rates and a positive organizational culture.

> Naturally, we see the world through our lens, and it is easily influenced by firsthand experiences.

In conclusion, our continuous effort is to learn "how" to effectively leverage diversity and inclusion. By engaging a diverse workforce, we are uncovering the answers to the "how" directly from our team members. A diverse workforce is not just a moral imperative; it is a strategic necessity for businesses striving to thrive in the 21st century. The benefits extend far beyond the office walls, positively impacting innovation, problem-solving, and corporate reputation. Embracing diversity is not simply the right thing to do; it is a fundamental driver of success in our interconnected and ever-evolving business landscape.

Inclusion is where the magic happens . . .

CHAPTER FIVE

Stories of Change and Where It's Still Needed

Innovation:

- **Understanding** that we can walk alongside people as they re-enter society and the workforce can change the future of work. People do not need to do it alone. People are built for connection and when we support our workforce they will build and carry on the business.. Companies should start addressing needs by putting people first and changing the way business runs!
- **Vulnerability** is a strength. When men and women are willing to narrate their past so they can know better and do better, it is a leaders responsibility to respond and not react.
- **Addressing social needs** in employment means connecting with people to meet their needs. Sometimes individuals have had past hardships in their lives. This is not something to be taken lightly. It is real.

It is necessary to have systems of support in our workplaces that do not minimize individuals based on their needs. We cannot blame people or employers for what they do not know. The time of simply handing an EAP (Employee Assistance Program) flyer with a phone number has run it's course. This is not people first and can merely be a band-aide gesture.

Vulnerability and transparency are strengths not weaknesses. When we take that approach wholistically to offer support, it nurtures a people-first culture, and rehumanizes employment. Notice the "w" added to holistic. I want employers to consider the importance of focusing on the wholeness of the employee. When we proactively rehumanize our workplaces to focus on the dimensions of wellness we will truly become people-first workplaces. Addressing the hard times employees face with patience and grit can greatly change company culture and positively impact employee retention.

Before taking on this work, I was not aware of the impact trauma has on people's lives. It seems to be the place people get stuck. I teach Career Discovery in the Black Hawk County Jail. I know my class may merely be a distraction for the inmates. It is always my hope that they leave with a better sense of understanding themselves and what types of employment are the best fit for them.

While there, I also want the men to know community-based service providers, leaders in our community, and local organizations want to see true reform in the criminal justice system. I usually share about our work in the community. It takes time to build a level of trust when working inside a place where people are held under supervision.

Since addressing trauma seems to be an area that strongly correlates with marginalized people, I speak about it in class. Frequently, I discuss One City United's vision of achieving criminal justice reform and my aspiration to foster increased collaboration between the Department of Corrections and community-based programs.

> In one of my classes, I made the statement "I do not believe we will see true reform in criminal justice until we start to address ACEs (Adverse Childhood Experiences). I had no idea the impact that statement would have on my class. It opened my eyes to a powerful realization.

The following week, at the end of class, a man sitting at the front table said, "Hey, you wanna hear something funny?" Expecting an actual joke, I responded, "Sure." Instead, he revealed, "Wanna hear how my life of crime began? When I was 5 years old, my dad equipped me with cameras and sent me crawling through the doggie doors of wealthy homes so he could case each house."

I had no idea how to respond. There was silence. Then immediately, the man sitting next to him took his hand and slapped him on the upper arm and said, "I got one for ya!" He went on to explain, "When I turned

12, my dad wanted to show me that I was a man; so he stuck a needle in my arm. I have been an addict ever since!"

I was speechless and had a strong sense that I needed to lean in and listen, to better understand. The silence seemed to be a necessary reaction of respect for the vulnerability shared. You could have heard a pin drop.

Re-read this if it was hard to imagine. Let it resonate and soak in because it still impacts me to this day.

Trauma in people's lives surfaces in different ways. Workplaces that provide safe and transparent environments encourage clear communication and transparency without judgment based on past experiences. When challenges arise, companies can assist by having a plan.

Some environments shut down people's ability to work through problems/trauma. Others empower people to work through and overcome.

Terry

I do not want to paint a picture that everything is beautiful, (Pollyanna perfect) or that we are "fixing people." I like to say, "hurt people hurt people" and "healed people heal people."

It is quite frankly hard, challenging, and sometimes painful to hear what people have been through. It is not pretty. I have been putting off writing this because it's hard to say goodbye.

I met Terry when his niece stopped at a weekly One City outreach location when I was serving food. For two years we had outreaches with volunteers from six churches. It helped us to know our community better and its struggles.

I had known Liza for years, from working with kids in ATEV. Liza pulled me aside at an outreach and wanted to talk about her Uncle Terry. She shared that her uncle Terry was struggling and had come home from being incarcerated for 25 years and could not find employment. She inquired in a hopeful and assuring sort of way, "You help people coming out of prison to find jobs, right?"

Nobody would hire Terry. He was older and he'd been out of prison for eight months without a job. He was living with his sister Sarah, Liza's mom, and was starting to get discouraged.

As I am writing this, I am preparing to go to Terry's funeral. Today we will be celebrating Terry's life. I consider it an honor to have gotten to be a little part of the last couple of years of his life.

After Terry graduated Momentum, he and his sister would come to every event and graduation possible to encourage perfect strangers in their life transformation journey. Terry believed in God, and he knew what it took for him to change. Terry knew it was God who changed him truly, but he had to put in the work for himself. He had to take on real and perceived barriers. When Terry stopped attending graduations, I knew something was wrong. Terry had cancer throughout his body and did not know it.

I accepted Terry into Momentum Term 5, after interviewing him and hearing his frustrations about how the world had changed and how he couldn't find a job. His term was a bit challenging for me as we were still social distancing because of COVID-19. We had terrible acoustics in our space, which made it difficult for people with hearing impairments, like Terry, to receive what we were saying.

I sat Terry at the front table. He was a tall broad-shouldered, older man who looked natural in cowboy-style attire. He had the sweetest personality. He was quiet. Terry did not talk a lot in class. Momentum is not programmatic but rather its foundation is built on relationships. I thought early on, "How am I going to know if I am even reaching this man because he is just so darn quiet?" "Will I ever be able to get him a job?" "Will ageism along with a violent criminal record make it impossible?"

Doubt kept creeping in on me because Terry had done some things that seemed so out of character. Especially compared to the person who sat in my classroom. I was ashamed of myself for thinking this way because of my faith in Jesus Christ. It is a human flaw to judge others based on their past actions.

So much had changed in Terry's 25 years of being in prison: technology, social media, cell phones, computers, and even how to apply for jobs. Terry's sister, Sarah, who was no spring chicken herself, would drive him to One City each day. It was nearly a 30-minute drive one way. She was invested in seeing her brother find purposeful employment.

As time passed, Terry started to trust I would not judge him based on his past. He was a true gentle giant with a quiet and calming personality. His presence made me feel comfortable. I just never knew what he was taking in from each class.

What we do at Momentum is build relationships and empower people through self-actualization and education in what is typically called "soft skills." I believe we can teach people the technical skills to complete work tasks, but if they do not have these soft skills, how will they retain employment on a bad day?

Terry had those bad days and had burnt employers repeatedly before going to prison. Terry was a human resource nightmare on paper.

Momentum is a community-based program with many volunteer facilitators who share their stories of adversity. While they teach crucial life-changing topics, they also identify what it took for their lives to change. This helps participants realize they are not alone.

Terry had a supportive family which many people with mental health, recovery, and reentry stigmas can use up. Terry stayed after class, doing volunteer projects many days: painting walls at One City, creating a coffee bar area, and cleaning. I called in reinforcements from my friend, Doug, who had worked with returning citizens at Iowa Works.

Doug excels at what I refer to as "mining for gold in people" - a process of identifying and uncovering their skills, assets, and hidden abilities that may not be immediately apparent.

For older individuals, particularly those who have experienced traumatic events or returning citizens who feel disconnected from society, a significant challenge lies in constructing a resume that accurately represents their skills and experience after so many years away from the workforce.

> 66 I want to thank you because I have been addicted to meth all my life and attended all kinds of drug treatment programs. It was Momentum that helped me stop.

It had been so long since Terry had worked and there were memories he did not want to reclaim as part of his past. Doug and I both had to get out our pickaxes to reach Terry's hidden treasures.

Through our classes Terry began to open up to me, sharing his deep-seated hurts. It was like peeling an onion back. I began to see that grief had inundated Terry's life as he shared the pain related to losing people he loved. He became addicted to drugs to mask that pain. He shared he had felt responsible for his little brother drowning because he was not there for him when it happened. A girlfriend died while he was incarcerated. Prison does not typically address grief, which is part of reform.

The impact Momentum made on Terry's life did not resonate with me until we celebrated his first 90 days of employment. Terry stood and looked at his plaque on our wall with all the other graduates. He pointed to his plaque and said "I want to thank you because I have been addicted to meth all my life and attended all kinds of drug treatment programs. It was Momentum that helped me stop." Terry was seeking change and received it. He was the first graduate from his class to obtain employment and it was back in the industry he loved, tree service, lawn care & snow removal for a local tree service.

At Terry's funeral, I heard the pastor preach the sermon about the prodigal son who came back to his community and was celebrated and accepted. His sister shared that when he attended a church, he was hurt deeply. Terry was treated like a leper instead of being welcomed home. We who claim Christianity are called to embrace the prodigal son and celebrate his homecoming. That did not happen for Terry, until he attended One City's Momentum. However, that did not stop Terry. He knew who he was, a great uncle who thoroughly enjoyed his niece's family. He had also gained an extended family and a community who loved him. Today, I say farewell but not forever to my friend Terry.

COMING FULL CIRCLE

Tommy

Tommy came to open enrollment for Momentum after I visited the Men's Residential Work Facility, several days before the Term 6 open enrollment. Attending open enrollment is a prerequisite to being accepted into Momentum.

Individuals must go through a two-step interview process before being considered for the classes. When I met Tommy, he was very defeated because he could not find employment. He'd applied to a lot of places, with no success. For most people, it was a good time to find employment because there was, and still is, an employment crisis. However, finding employment was not happening for Tommy. He was very frustrated at that point.

At Tommy's Momentum graduation, he shared that prior to meeting me, he was considering committing a parole violation that would send him back to prison. Tommy had been in prison 19 years and so much had changed in our society while he was incarcerated. He explained the first time he was allowed to take time away from the Department of Corrections work facility, he just sat on the front step and experienced a full-blown anxiety attack. Unfortunately, he did not know what that meant or where to go. He just sat there panicked until a residential officer came out to talk to him.

Tommy had anxiety about everything, once he was released into the men's facility. Taking the free time given to go for a walk seemed overwhelming. When we met, I could tell he was a very conscientious person and wanted to do things the right way. After 19 years of being told what to do, where to go, and developing his coping skills, he now had to acclimate to home.

During my visit with Tommy at the men's work facility he opened up about the numerous employment rejections he had faced from potential employers. He had been involved in an armed robbery and served 19 of 23 years in prison. While visiting, I learned he was downhearted and was getting depressed by rejection after rejection letter from employers. The thought of getting into something that would help him seemed to offer a glimmer of hope for a normal life outside the Department of Corrections.

He was admitted into Momentum Term 6, and it was like mining for the gold within Tommy. He had used his time inside prison walls to gain every certification along with knowledge that would help him when he was released. The more time I spent 1:1 with Tommy the more his abilities, strengths, and assets came to light. It was truly like mining for gold and Tommy had plenty of nuggets, showing that he used his time in prison wisely.

 When Tommy did get a job during the six weeks of Momentum; I realized his employer did not know the gold Tommy had inside of him.

Tommy's parents were very supportive while he was incarcerated. Many people do not have that kind of support. It turns out I had met his mother years prior, at the Iowa State Capitol for an Iowa Justice Action Network (IJAN) session with state legislators. She had shared her son's story with me over lunch and seemed very hopeful for the day he would be released. The Momentum Term was nearly over before I knew it was Tommy's story that I had heard years prior. It was a full-circle moment for me because Momentum had not been created yet.

When men are released to the Men's Work Facility, the top expectation for them is to find employment. Much of the time I hear people's P.O. (Parole Officer and/or Probation Officer) tell them "Just get a job." Unfortunately, it's common to hear about some employers taking advantage of men from work release, paying less knowing they have a captive workforce that can easily receive a violation. I do know people desire change when they commit to nearly 4 hours of class each day in Momentum followed up by 8 hours of work. That is what I witnessed with Tommy.

When Tommy did get a job during the six weeks of Momentum; I realized his employer did not know the gold Tommy had inside of him. I told him, "You should share your new and improved resume that showcases your skills and abilities." He did. The response he received from his supervisor was initially hopeful. But after the supervisor shared it with the the company owner, he was once again defeated, as the owner reacted, "There is no way he learned all this in prison!" That was the wrong response.

Before graduating from Momentum, Tommy had a manufacturing job offer making substantially more money. His employers realized they were about to lose a great employee.

You see, one of Tommy's top values is loyalty. He wanted to give his current employer a chance. It became a bidding war for Tommy's time. He eventually left the first company and has been employed with the other manufacturer ever since. The Operations Manager told me that Tommy described his time in my class this way, "One City's Momentum is an emotional boot camp, and it saved my life."

The Catfishing Hustle

While in prison, Tommy experienced a significant loss. His girlfriend who died and he had a lot of grief to process during his time in Momentum. Prisons do not typically staff grief counselors. This is a topic we cover to help people address loss and trauma. Tommy was lonely.

When he was in Momentum, other participants called it to my attention "Tommy is being catfished!" Tommy had no clue with all the changes in technology that those handheld computers, (aka cell phones), can lead to being scammed. The internet can be a dangerous place.

Tommy's mom even called me exclaiming, "I think these women contacting Tommy are taking his money! Can you help him understand what is happening?"

For those of you who don't know what catfishing, it is a common criminal hustle on the internet. Tommy spent his time in prison learning skills to have a new hustle. He didn't understand this new technology where people reach out over the internet. He did not know they were not who they were perceived to be. He also didn't know they would build a relationship through conversations, texts, and emails. The time would always come for them to ask for money, for some reason or another.

I did speak to Tommy about these "so-called women." I think I told him, "This is probably some fifty-year-old, overweight, man sitting in his underwear, on a computer or burner phone, trying to take your money." Even at Tommy's Momentum graduation, he was sure this lady was coming from Texas to be there. I was nearly positive she would not show up. Turns out Tommy was being catfished!

Another full circle moment happened when Tommy came as a graduate, to give back by speaking to a Momentum class. Every group of participants has unique stories. Tommy's story of life transformation, after being in prison 19 years took his classmates' excuses away. In that class, I was able to introduce Tommy to a young lady who had an old hustle of catfishing men on the internet. Tommy turned a couple of shades of pink and was embarrassed when I introduced him to Ella, who explained her daily illegal activity along with the ins and outs of the scam of catfishing. Fortunately, Ella changed her life as well and found a NEW hustle! She achieved her lifelong goal of working in healthcare.

Tommy's mom re-introduced him to his high school sweetheart, Tori. She is the love of Tommy's life. Trust me, it did not take long for Tori to clean out Tommy's little black book of phone contacts. Their wedding was the first Momentum graduate's wedding we were invited to attend. Those firsts are really special events! Tommy has legitimized his NEW hustle: he works at the same manufacturing company who saw his value after Momentum. He is married to the love of his life Tori, is now off parole, and celebrated with a family vacation to Hawaii with his extended new family.

Cam & the New Hustle

My passion and purpose revolves around reform and acclimating returning citizens home from jail or prison. I began connecting with Cam from inside the prison walls months before he was released/paroled became the initial inroad for One City's Momentum. Cam had gone to jail 57 times and was considered a frequent flier or in correction terms a "habitual offender," by sheriff deputies. Cam went to prison for the first time at age 16. He spent a total of 14 years in state and federal prisons.

Cam heard about Momentum through his daughter's mom Stacey. She connected me to Cam through the great work done by Iowa Works Career Counselor, Brian, at Rockwell City Prison. When he paroled, I knew Cam would need employment immediately, so I called Schad West, Operations Manager, at Kay Park Industries in Janesville, Iowa. Cam was interviewed and hired for a welding position.

The full circle momentum for me was when Cam reached the life transformational classes of Momentum. It gets intense during these classes. People can look introspectively at their lives, choices, and mistakes. At this point, they start to own it all and develop emotional intelligence they never developed before.

> " Cam then said, "I am sorry because I was the reason he kept relapsing. I was his drug dealer!"

One morning, Cam approached me and asked if we could talk in private, in my office. I knew he had been working crazy hours, without missing a Momentum class session, so I was prepared for him to say something like, "This is getting to be too much." Instead, Cam said, "I want to tell you that I am sorry."

"For what?" I responded.

Cam followed with, "Remember when George lived with you guys, and he kept relapsing?"

I said, "Yes" in a very interested manner, leaning in to understand, and pausing to ponder what he would say next. George was one of the young men who had lived with us. He, like Cam, was also a frequent flier to the system (in and out of jail and prisons).

Cam then said, "I am sorry because I was the reason he kept relapsing. I was his drug dealer!"

This was absolutely a full circle moment for me! My response was most likely very shocking to Cam. I'm sure he didn't what to expect and probably thought I was going to be furious at what he had just revealed. I was elated because a program I had fought hard to bring to the Cedar Valley had inadvertently made such a change in Cam that he felt true remorse. That is when I realized Momentum was creating what I dubbed a "New Hustle" for people seeking life transformation. Momentum was changing lives where people were laying down their old hustles and vices, and legitimizing their new hustles. In this case Cam had identified the harm he had done. He wanted to be forgiven.

I celebrated that day because I knew that one drug dealer who had negatively impacted my household by dealing drugs to our friend George would no longer be in "the life." When George comes out of prison my hope is that he would also seek to legitimize a "New Hustle." But one thing I knew for sure that day, is that Cam found himself a new hustle.

Cam is still working through some things he had never faced before, like traumatic childhood experiences. I believe with some good counseling, as well as his faith and trust in God, he can heal. He connected to a great church, Hope City, right away when he came out of prison. I connected him to a mentor, who also attends Hope City Church and is also a retired police officer. His wife is a retired P.O. After Cam's first time hanging out with them, he exclaimed, "You'll never guess what I did this weekend?!! I watched football with a cop and his wife who was a P.O. and I liked it . . ." Cam and Stacey continue to be involved and volunteer time, through their church, with a group called Rise Up. Cam found out he had already reached journeyman welder status when in Momentum. He continues as a welder for one of our international corporations. Cam has led others to Momentum including his best friend. He will tell you he still has challenges, traumas and giants to face. I spent a significant time listening to the childhood trauma Cam remembers; that not even his family knows. It takes time to process and heal. This is why community is important!

Full Circle: George came out of prison recently. He heard about the changes people are making in their lives. I think he was more curious than anything. Not everyone makes it through Momentum the first time because it is an emotional bootcamp. It is my hope I see George embrace the chutzpah (another word for audacity) to face his fears and embrace change for good.

These are men returning from incarceration. People can change when given the opportunity.

Julie

When Julie came to Momentum she was told by her P.O. Terrance, "You don't need Momentum, just get a job." He'd supported her in drug court, so it confused her when he didn't understand the value of a community-based program like Momentum. We shared that over the years there have been many fly-by-night programs. They had all dwindled away. The Department of Corrections was not used to seeing organizations be consistent. She would need to teach Terrance by showing him. She did just that and since Terrance has sent others to One City's Momentum.

Julie had more than her criminal background of 20 felonies stacked up against her. She also had cancer of the spleen. Her Momentum term 13 was the first class that was hit hard by sickness. For goodness sake, we made it through two years of a worldwide pandemic without a single case of COVID-19, the flu, or any other viruses. Julie's term was different. Everything hit us. Julie was tenacious and did not yield when things became strenuous for her. It seemed to become a challenge to her perseverance.

Julie's heart's desire was to work in the healthcare field and advance her education to become a forensic pathologist. Unfortunately, with the punitive nature of our state, Julie learned Iowa would not be a state that welcomed her with open arms as an employee. It is ironic to me, because many of Iowa's legislators are known for their conservative Christian values. The Bible that I know and love, illustrates that all lives can change and be transformed.

When graduating from Momentum, Julie had multiple options for employment. She recently spoke to a Momentum class stating, "I always wanted to work in the healthcare field, but due to my felonies, I never thought it would be possible for me." Julie was strongly pursued by one of our local hospitals. The Human Resource Director attended graduation as well as her very supportive PO Terrance.

ALL LIVES CAN CHANGE!

#WCL

All was great until the background check came back with the 20 felonies that she was required to disclose. Even the one that dated back twenty-some years. This can be a very arduous task even for someone with just a few felonies. Julie called me in tears because she was forced to recall and explain every single difficult time of her life. I explained to her that this is due diligence.

Explaining everything ended up taking Julie nearly four days of writing about the events that had taken place in her life. She did it with fortitude, taking accountability for what she had done in every instance.

On the positive side, she narrated her transformative journey, taking credit for her efforts through self-reflection and the skills she acquired during her time in drug court with Terrance. This was followed by the intense emotional boot camp experience she went through with One City's Momentum program.

Allie

When I met Allie, she had hopes of getting into Momentum for the life transformation it could bring. She relocated to Waterloo to begin a new life. For some people, it works best to get outta town and start over. Allie did just that.

She was from a city a few hours away from Waterloo. She thought everything was going to be smooth sailing, then reality hit. She learned there are people who will try to take advantage of the those returning from prison and that is what was happening.

When she moved here, she was accepted into a transitional house that was not as it seemed. After moving in, she realized what was really going on. Another participant from the same Momentum term who was living there also shared a similar story with me. These ladies were moving in for support.

Overnight, Allie realized she had made a huge mistake and saw the toxic signs. She became homeless by making a good choice to leave and was going to be on the streets. This would mean an automatic violation and back to prison she would go. We worked extremely hard to bridge this gap, being transparent with the Department of Corrections and advocating for Allie.

During Momentum, we spend a tremendous amount of time connecting individuals to the resources they need for success. I remember the conversation clearly, Allie calling me sobbing, "I don't know what I'm going to do Michele! I had to get out of that place!" I responded, "I'm on my way!"

As I turned the corner, I saw her small body lugging most of her belongings as she walked down the street, away from a place that was not a good place for any returning citizen to live.

Allie had no place to go, but she did know that if she got out of that phony housing front, she would be alright. The One City staff dedicated time to facilitating the connections she needed in Waterloo. They assisted her in obtaining mental health and recovery counseling services, reached out to the local women's shelter to secure housing for her, and maintained communication with her probation officer, who was located out of town.

It was crucial that I could assure him that Allie had a community of support and Momentum was going to bridge this unforeseen gap. Eventually, Allie was able to get into a great sober living environment for women.

Life has never been easy for Allie. At 11 years old she was forced to learn how to manufacture meth. At 19, she was blown up in a meth lab. Talk about resilience . . . Allie exemplified a toughness of spirit I have never seen before. The definition "Quitter" is not in this lady's dictionary. She made it through Momentum with a stick-to-it attitude that was just plain impressive.

After Momentum Allie, knew she wanted to pursue higher education and desired to become a peer support specialist and get a degree in trauma-informed care. I watched her start to check these things off her list including getting a driver's license and a car, for the first time. She calls it as she sees it and isn't scared to challenge the status quo.

Full Circle for Julie and Allie became a Mother's Day Gift to Remember

Julie is continuing her studies and researching the two states that will hire her to be a Forensic Pathologist. She continues her work in environmental services for the same hospital.

Allie continues her studies in trauma-informed care. The last I heard, she was on the Dean's list. They both recently came to speak to One City's Term 16 of Momentum. These ladies take away excuses by sharing their stories of overcoming adversities and encouraging soon-to-be graduates to live their best lives.

I received a call from my friend Kam Middlebrook from Reform Alliance on Friday, May 12th, 2023, around 4 pm. Kam asked, "Do you have any women who would be blessed by a special Mother's Day gift?" Granted, it was 4 pm on the Friday before Mother's Day. I responded, "Of course we do!"

I made some calls and confirmed I could share the contact information for Julie and Allie. The ladies called me Saturday Mother's Day Eve and shared, "Reform Alliance is going to pay our supervision fees, fines, and court costs!" Both women had a substantial amount, and never could have fathomed such generosity!

There were 50 women nationwide who were blessed and given an unconditional monetary form of love that could boost their ability to enhance their lives. Two were chosen from Momentum graduates. The debt they cleared totaled around $20,000 for each woman.

This was a dream come true for both women, as they'd been pursuing their educational goals despite this mounting debt. Reform Alliance took on this thoughtful task of wiping out their debt.

I believe by creating a path to opportunity, we can start to eradicate poverty, which in turn creates safer communities. This act of unconditional kindness gave two productive citizens, who are also Momentum graduates, a future forward.

Thank you to Reform Alliance, Michael Rubin, and Kim Kardashian for making dreams into a reality!

Graduates Come Full Circle Too

We have impacted so many lives that now things come full circle for graduates too. What I mean is, life can assist us all in seeing how far we have come, when we allow ourselves to continually grow. We can begin to see the benefits of our own growth through the work others put into their lives.

I remember a Momentum graduation where one man stood out. During classes, I could see he wasn't sure about this whole life transformation thing. Our classroom coordinator even helped him get employment during the term. His Parole Officer was pleased. This class was memorable. Most of the class was in recovery, including this gentleman. I will refer to him as "Dumplin," his street name. This class had its definite challenges. A lot of people did not make it through. The ones that did have done great things and the majority have continued with life transformation.

When I shared the Momentum stages of change, one participant was so convicted in her heart that she handed over her drugs during the break. Trust me, when something like that happens authorities have no clue what to do with it!

Dumplin had his challenges as well. I do not think he had ever considered change before as we approach it.

Dumplin

In class, I pointed out that many individuals on our wall have successfully graduated, became gainfully employed, and had an old hustle. They had an old hustle that ended with them being incarcerated.

I shared that I knew we were making a difference when the county prosecutor stopped to visit a year prior and said he knew over 80% of the folks on the wall. That day Dumplin started taking the opportunity of getting a "new hustle" to heart. He seemed to get serious, wanting to do better for his kids and family. Little did I know. Two of his daughters had been in my youth group when I was a youth group leader.

At graduation, Dumplin was called up by the classroom coordinator and she introduced him by his street name Dumplin. He shared how he had two employment opportunities. He could have worked in the culinary arts for two separate employers. They both wanted him and offered him jobs the same day. At graduation, Dumplin talked about Momentum giving him the skills to have a "new hustle".

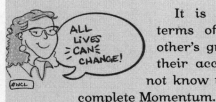

It is common to have many different terms of Momentum graduates attending other's graduations. They want to celebrate their accomplishments, even when they do not know the people because it is not easy to complete Momentum.

The self-reflection and introspective part of Momentum promotes choices that move individuals toward healing their life's traumas. This may be the hardest part of Momentum. It may be the first thing individuals have ever accomplished!

As I socialized and had some cake, two past graduates were visiting when I approached them. One said, "We didn't even recognize Dumplin. He used to be my drug dealer!" The other said, "Mine too!" That was a full circle moment for those grads; realizing how precious their sobriety was and how far they had come.

Unfortunately, Dumplin did not stay the course. I did everything I could to encourage and assist him. This included attending a PO appointment with him. The reason I attended was to explain how he had opportunities, and that it was up to him to move them forward.

When people truly want a new hustle, they will grasp onto those opportunities with gratitude and a desire to never return to the old life. Just narrating his past for a background check seemed to overwhelm Dumplin where he abandoned both employment opportunities.

I ran into Dumplin's daughter recently. She said, "I heard my dad graduated from your program." Then she shared who her dad was. It made me sad because for Dumplin, the streets were too strong.

I know his daughter wants to see life outside of incarceration work for her dad because he is not "Dumplin" to her. He is "dad."

She did give me a thought to ponder and that was the *why* ... behind the reason the streets were too strong. She said, "The problem is my dad knows most of his check will be automatically garnished with so many children and back child support."

It's not that Dumplin is unwilling to support his children. The problem lies in the lack of opportunities to start over in a way that pays the bills, allowing these parents to choose a better way of life that promotes self-efficacy.

Unfortunately, the policy rules and doesn't always take in account the ramifications of it's action. There is a disconnect between policy and where empowers the people to move forward.

Hopefully, our lawmakers can take this to heart when they amend laws.

Heads up on Recovery and Mental Health

At Momentum, we understand the difficulty that can arise in supporting people in their recovery and mental health. It is challenging for them. It is challenging for us as well.

Have we been disappointed by individuals who have made bad choices? Yes. Have you? Yes, I'm quite sure you have, because you are reading this book.

We have seen people revert back to their old ways of doing life after Momentum. It's hard to be part of a solution when people forget there is a problem and aren't willing to get to the core of it.

Human Resource pre-employment processes are hard. Does it frustrate me? Yes. Does it frustrate you? Probably.

Folks, I am telling you, give some grace and patience. This "Hire slow, fire fast" human resource model isn't working. We get you!

Are you fully staffed? You are losing great candidates. People need jobs and if you are losing them before you even send an offer, you might need to look at your processes.

You might need to look at your website application. Review the support and direction you provide before having them narrate their past mistakes, so people understand your processes. You might also need to investigate your application and pre-employment screening. You are losing great people with potential. We get you!

We realized the power of building a fellowship through Momentum when we started seeing some drug relapses and individuals having challenges with their mental health. These two things can coincide. Both can occur simultaneously for those who are justice impacted and re-entered citizens. Do not let this deter you. People can change.

People can also have setbacks and need additional support. We needed to learn this. Have we experienced people not getting back up? Unfortunately, yes. I do not believe this book would have much credibility with you if everything at One City has always been just "hunky dory." Has it been at your workplace? No. This is where we are reminded that "people are human," and we must use their life stories on our journey to encourage and guide employers to rehumanize employment! We get you!

 People can also have setbacks and need additional support. We needed to learn this.

Have we lost people? Yes. Here is where I can allow my emotions to be worn on my sleeve. I have chosen not to mention names as this is personal and very hard on families who have lost loved ones who are in recovery. Currently, we have had three graduates who have passed away:

- **The first:** He had relapsed the week after his Momentum graduation. He did not show up to follow up on employment opportunities with me. I and his counselor, who referred him to our program, took him to the hospital and he was admitted because he started drinking again. After being released he did it all over again, fell, and passed away. Life can be hard. I remember listening to him when he was drunk talking about abuse. He had not worked through what was tormenting him. Life can be hard.
- **The second:** I received a call from the employer where our graduate worked. She loved her job there. They loved her. The manager notified me that she was found in the house of an ex-boyfriend and died of an apparent heart attack. She

had an oppressive life and grew up in poverty. She relocated to Waterloo from Chicago. She had previously had a stroke which was evident in her abilities. Her sole desire was to live independently, in a place she could call home, where her son and granddaughter would have the option to visit her, with the possibility of relocating to our city permanently.

- This graduate became homeless while she was in Momentum because her boyfriend did not like the growth, independence, and strides forward she was making. I assisted her in getting into a shelter, followed by a women's transitional house. I had seen tremendous growth in this beautiful older woman and so did her employer. Life can be hard.
- **The Third:** was our friend Terri, who I previously shared his story of change. Terri most likely had cancer when he was incarcerated and did not know it.

Have we seen individuals have mental health crises? Yes.

Connection matters: A graduate was in a toxic relationship and his girlfriend was not sober and he did not remain sober. However, he reached out for help. Through the great work of 911, a mobile crisis unit, and the Police Department this graduate bounced back quickly. He remembered what was shared in class about suicide prevention and reached out for help. Since he was willing to face mental health challenges and address where he was lacking in the dimensions of wellness, I have seen a great turnaround in his life. Full circle: He is now hiring Momentum graduates to work in the trades in the manufacturing industry.

Gaps: We have seen two graduates fall in the gap due to our country's healthcare system. They both had aged out of being under their parents' insurance and went without medication. Both had a healthcare crisis as they were without much needed medication. This disrupts peoples ability to retain employment. Healthcare should not be limited. We should not have this gap in a country as wealthy as America.

One bounced back and became employed by a state agency and the other is applying for disability services and gave up on employment at this point.

NOT BUSINESS AS USUAL

What have we learned and what are we doing differently? After seeing an individual relapse, I struggled and asked myself, "What do we need to do differently?" For the first year and a half, we had a zero-recidivism rate. That means not one justice-impacted individual returned to prison or jail.

When we lost someone to drug relapse and imprisonment, I had to ask myself: How could we have helped prevent this? I learned he had relapsed during the holidays. It was the anniversary of his mother's passing. The grief became too much to bear alone. I reached out to one of our social service leaders and inquired, "Who would best present the topic of Grief at Momentum?" That is when Cedar Valley Hospice entered the scene and started addressing grief in our space. This has been an amazing experience that has helped me better understand the significant trauma that people in our community have had to endure.

Although our grief education programs at Momentum were transformative for many participants, something was still missing in our ability to fully support people through their journey.

The answer seemed to go back to Peer Support. People need to know they are not alone. It did not take very many discussions with our board at One City to determine that having a Peer Support Group was needed.

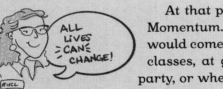

At that point, we were over two years into Momentum. We only saw graduates when they would come in to share with other Momentum classes, at graduations, at a special holiday party, or when they wanted assistance seeking better employment options. We have since enacted a Peer Support Group every week where we bring in guest speakers, share updates about each other's lives, and fellowship over a meal.

We also bring service providers in to speak about additional opportunities and encourage graduates to give input on additional speakers. I'm telling you even things as simple as decorating Christmas cookies were extremely supportive as well as being a new experience for one of our immigrant graduates.

The peer group on holiday stress was impactful and facilitated by an unlikely service provider - Alternatives. They reached out to us. There are organizations in our community offering supportive services that are great partners that can give a much-needed perspective.

WHERE COMPANIES MISSED THE MARK

Several graduates from our program, who are in recovery themselves, secured employment at a manufacturing company where many current employees are also in recovery. The challenge I am seeing is based on the adage, "all it takes is one bad apple to ruin a bunch."

When a company decides to be inclusive but has no follow through with supportive services, there will be challenges and retention will be hard. Peer Support is a great option for building accountability and a supportive service within the workplace. Dean will ask employers, "Wouldn't you rather have 38 really productive work hours versus 40 unproductive hours from your employees?"

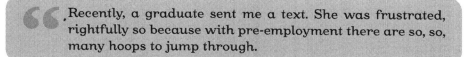

Recently, a graduate sent me a text. She was frustrated, rightfully so because with pre-employment there are so, so, many hoops to jump through.

After Momentum, it's been difficult for some since they received six weeks of solid support in a group setting, then it is time to get a job. Using the analogy of the mother bird kicking her baby birds out of the nest . . . Sometimes, I have to be like a mother bird.

Dean would say "Gutt it up buttercup!" and straightforwardly explain there is due diligence in everything you do in life; employment is one of those things.

Recently, a graduate sent me a text. She was frustrated, rightfully so because with pre-employment there are so, so, many hoops to jump through. After narrating her past to the Department of Human Services, and addressing additional related questions, she found herself engaged in a prolonged text conversation about flu shots she had taken and other ancillary details. This drawn-out process delayed getting to the point where she could receive a job offer and begin the orientation process for her new role.

I tell our graduates- *It is worth it! Trust the process!* I had to laugh when she sent me a text and called it a "scam". She was ready to throw in the towel, per se. This mother bird did not respond to her "scam" text. Guess what? She found her wings and came in to tell me she flew through the minutiae of the pre-employment trivial details.

LIFE HAPPENS: WHY NOT HEAD OFF JOB LOSS?

There is a level of transparency needed in the workplace. Many companies have not yet adopted a wholistic approach to their employment practices. As a co-founder of a nonprofit going into its toddler phase; having benefits and being competitive in the workplace can be challenging. A One City staff person recently shared, "It can be challenging when we place graduates into companies with better benefits and pay than we offer." We lay out what we can offer in advance, and we are continually improving and advancing. We are continually researching what other companies are doing. We want our staff to be vulnerable and allow us to be so as well. People work at One City because they love the results and the feeling of accomplishment when we can help individuals better themselves.

Can we do better? Always.

Do we face some of the same challenges you do? Most likely.

Are we learning how we can do better in supporting our staff? Absolutely.

Clear concise communication and expectations are vital for a mutually healthy work environment.

> ALL LIVES CAN CHANGE!
>
> A graduate reached out for assistance in seeking another position after losing his job. The employer called me after it was too late. The employer indicated that our graduate had been missing work and would be losing employment. That employer did not take the time to find out what was really going on.

This man had been an excellent employee. He was trained to take the place of machining equipment that a lifelong tenured employee had done with great proficiency. I was told, all of a sudden, he was calling in. The employer did not know why. The employer did not open the door for conversation as to why.

This Momentum graduate was experiencing what many Americans in the "sandwich generation" are experiencing. His mother had been put in a long-term care facility because she had dementia. He was watching his mother dwindle away before his eyes because she was not eating at mealtime. He had to go to the nursing home to feed her so she would eat, and he also had a young son to raise on his own.

Could a conversation change the trajectory of his plight? What if the human resource department had been tasked with finding out "the why" for changes in his work performance? When employers take the time to get to root cause, money is saved and time is managed well. What would have happened had he been given an option of a split shift or another shift?

 What would have happened had he been given the ability to be transparent with life issues?

What would have happened if he had been given the ability to be transparent with life issues? The time for hypermasculinity in manufacturing has made its course for being effective. We need to bring human resource management back. This generation expects more.

When we put people and their needs first, in employment, production will not suffer. It will increase.

How about we allow for vulnerability in the workplace related to being specific about expectations, not just at onboarding but when issues arise? I believe our employees, work environments, and harmony in the workplace are worth taking the time to ask and receive feedback. Then act on the feedback. Can you imagine the financial savings? I can.

As a leader, every conversation, meeting, and encounter is a chance to inspire, motivate, and uplift those around you.

~ Gifford Thomas

Partnering with Kay Park and Recreation happened through meeting their leadership team at a Reverse Career Fair. Kay Park began hiring Momentum graduates. The satisfaction of the staff we spoke to at Kay Park was off the charts!

A man reached out to me from prison because he knew he needed Momentum and wanted his life to be different when he returned home. I knew he had all the skills that would be appreciated at Kay Park in Janesville, Iowa. I also knew he would not be judged for his past, as they assume good intent. I also knew that he would be working in a supportive business model. My next step was to call Schad West, Operations Manager. Kay Park rarely has job openings due to their great company culture as well as having an innovative and inclusive work environment. When touring Kay Park for the first time, we foresaw a wonderful collaborative relationship emerging. What Dean and I found out was that we have a common passion and purpose to rehumanize employment and create people-first cultures. We can all glean knowledge and understanding from their business model. Kay Park and Recreation was started and continues to grow as a multi-generational innovative business model of the Borglum family.

CHAPTER SIX

Kay Park Industries

WE TRUST OUR TEAM TO GET IT RIGHT

Kay Park and Recreation was founded in 1954 by an entrepreneur, opportunist, problem solver, and visionary named Keith Borglum. In 2024, his sons Chris and Larry will celebrate the 70th year of operation as the owners, in the same purposeful visionary style as their father.

Their line of commercial recreational equipment such as picnic tables, grills, benches, and even mobile bleachers is manufactured right here in Janesville, Iowa. Back in 1964, they also began producing above-ground UL-certified storage tanks to diversify and expand the product lines.

In 2016, when Keith retired at the age of 90, Chris and Larry took on the task of modernizing and growing the business further through multiple strategies. The most important of which was to continue expanding on a true People First culture.

> By caring about our people, and investing in their development through extensive cross-training and outside resources, our team gives back.

As Chris and Larry set to chart a path forward, it was imperative to them to set a foundation that represented what Kay was, is, and will become. From this came the first version of the core values. As the company experienced high sales volumes, the addition of some new staff, and changes in the supply chain, those core values were revised in 2021 to what they are today.

1) People First
2) Trust
3) Kay Team
4) Getting it Right is More Important Than Being Right.

It is through the lens of these values that Kay orchestrates its unique ability to bring in and cultivate talent, along with growing and enhancing the existing team. The underlying drivers of the People First value are the belief that it starts with providing a living, a fulfilling environment, personal development combined with flexibility, valuing one another, and having an emotional investment in long-term relationships. Along with the understanding that we will never sacrifice you, your well-being, or your development for the sake of running the business. Or as Chris and Larry like to summarize the values, "We trust our team to get it right."

"By caring about our people, and investing in their development through extensive cross-training and outside resources, our team gives back."

Loyalty is still very much alive at Kay, and it goes both ways. By allowing their team to keep themselves, their families, and loved ones as a priority, they experience very little turnover. Employees are energized by what the company is doing and they understand the "why."

Kay Park consistently provides transparency through short- and long-term strategy sharing. Whether it be about the seasonal nature of some of the products and the effects it has on production, to capital investments in the business. The team must know all of this ahead of time.

Company leaders are coached to "actively seek" opportunities to lead, coach, and mentor. Waiting for people to come to you with a problem means you are already behind.

Kay Park keeps their engagement high by providing an open dialogue atmosphere. Whether at the safety meetings, financial literacy classes, or day-to-day as everyone works together. They talk. Production can stop for a few minutes as leaders stay close to the team and work with them to solve the issues that come up.

When Keith started business in the local community it began as a traditional one-shift operating from 6:30 AM to 5 PM. Over time and drastically changing economic conditions, it became clear that to overcome the farm crisis, and then an 18-month backlog, something had to change. The Park portion of the business was growing rapidly, which was the catalyst for introducing flexible scheduling and creative shift times.

From 2009 through 2019, they used hiring through Temp agencies to find new employees. Fast forward to today. The core of the belief in flexible scheduling still exists and is thriving at Kay.

Amidst the challenges posed by the COVID-19 pandemic, rapidly rising inflation, and the difficulty in attracting new employees, it became necessary to leverage our strengths and combine them with a

 Employees are energized by what the company is doing and they understand the "why."

labor force that faces significant barriers to employment.

It was a chance meeting at a Reverse Career Fair where we first met Michele Feltes and the One City Momentum program. As we shared insights, challenges, and understanding, it was apparent that working together would be an alignment that could have positive effects on the community and the business.

You see, our flexible schedule consists of picking your own start time and leave time. There isn't a points system or discipline for running a few minutes late. All they ask is that the employee simply call in and let them know if they aren't going to make it or will be significantly late. That's it. Nothing complicated. Life comes first, then work.

In 2019 Chris saw the need to create a hiring process versus using outside agencies. He understood the importance of hiring for culture fit and enlisting their employees to create and execute a specific hiring practice.

As they became more active in the community and spent more time at One City, something became very clear. They realized that IF they wanted to show what the company was all about as a business, they needed to widen the scope of how they hired new employees.

Kay Park had previously listed jobs for "Welders," "Painters," or "Fabricators" when what they were actually looking for, first, was the

 They also became better teachers as they pursued a path to higher levels of cross-training.

right cultural fit. They were looking for people that matched them in a behavioral sense, and not just some checklist of previous experiences.

They found that they had ample in-house talent that could emphasize their work culture in ads, instead of a specific skill set. They also became better teachers as they pursued a path to higher levels of cross-training. This approach aligns with the Momentum Program, which aims to equip individuals facing barriers with the tools and resources necessary to become the best version of themselves – the version they aspire to and are capable of becoming.

They realized that their hiring practices had been too narrowly focused. The Momentum program helped them understand that there was a broader pool of potential candidates that could be reached and considered for employment opportunities.

Don't get it wrong, there are times when specific skill sets are needed, but they didn't find that to be the overwhelming need. They believed that by taking the time to truly understand each person, including their level of emotional intelligence and dedication, they could more easily identify candidates whose values and qualities aligned with the business culture they hold in high regard.

Trust, as a core value, comes with some deeper understanding and meaning for Kay Park. One of the key points is "Assume Good Intent." That, in and of itself, lines up with the belief that people deserve second chances, and that just because they have experienced setbacks in the past doesn't mean that is what their future holds in store. Momentum offers that same principle. Assuming good intent doesn't mean you walk around with rose-colored glasses, or willful disregard for what's happening right in front of you.

"Assume Good Intent" means approaching situations with the belief that when you don't understand someone's actions or motivations, you should avoid reverting to past experiences, taking offense, or assuming they are wrong. Instead, it encourages being curious instead of judgmental, and empathetic rather than defensive. It prompts you to ask questions and seek a better understanding of the situation, rather than making negative assumptions.

Momentum and Kay both offer accountability through growth. It's within Kay's values that they are able to seek a higher level of understanding of themselves, each other, and the world itself.

Creating a People-First culture doesn't happen overnight, not with a new banner that says it, or without implementing real changes as to how your leadership and team members view and treat each other. For Kay, it all started with Keith Borglum. His unique perspective and dedication to serving the community around him with the job opportunities and the products they built.

Now Chris and Larry are carrying the torch that continues to light the path of community connection, second chances, and most importantly love and respect. What sets them apart is their dedication to forging a path for business growth through their team, embracing an approach that most others have shied away from.

Chris and Larry are consistently and openly lifelong learners. Understanding that change, while challenging at times, is best met head-on with unique solutions that keep people engaged and "all in."

Chris summarized it quite well when he recently asked, "How can other employers that want to change culture and hire people with barriers start?"

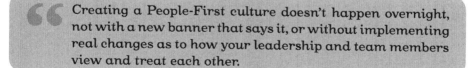

Creating a People-First culture doesn't happen overnight, not with a new banner that says it, or without implementing real changes as to how your leadership and team members view and treat each other.

He simply stated the obvious but difficult task, "You must meet them where they are now. Understand what they expect out of the relationship. They are all volunteers and should be treated as such. If you understand what their expectations are . . . what can YOU change, as an employer, to meet those expectations and still successfully meet your customer's needs as well?"

The world has changed significantly in 70 years. The challenges have been many, and complex at times. While the difficulties may have seemed insurmountable, at times, Kay Park's solution is a simple and meaningful one.

Living and working through a set of core values that will sustain you as a person and collectively as a business. That is the alignment Kay Park shares with Momentum.

Equipping people with the tools to thrive in an ever-changing environment without having to compromise yourself, your family, or your team.

"The more we tend to stick to the 'basics,' our Core Values, the further ahead we tend to stay. It's when we listen with the intent to understand, assume good intent, and trust each other to get it right that even our most daunting challenges can be overcome."

What we do at One City's Momentum is Unstuck People's Mind Stuckery!

~ Michele Feltes aka WCL

CHAPTER SEVEN
When Things Don't Go as Planned

Of course, there are days when it seems Flex has to be my middle name. Can you relate? Right when you think everything is going smooth, change blindsides you. That is when I know my middle name is FLEX. That is just how it is with employment. We must be flexible.

Every time you think you have seen it all something new arises. Does that sound familiar?

As an employer, we were not ready.

Is that something you say often? Is there always a new situation that causes you to have to punt or make a new plan, add a new policy, or procedure?

As an employer that does not feel good, does it?

We must do it too. We have found that we need to expand our training for upskilling individuals into professional roles.

I, myself, have learned, through working with individuals with barriers, that you cannot blame someone for not knowing what they do not know. It is unfortunate, but it is because nobody has ever taught them.

A good example would be educating individuals on the difference between hourly clock-in and clock-out positions and salaried positions. I have come to realize people do not really understand the difference between the two. That is why we are implementing a program within the Momentum Business Network to have professional mentors.

This begs the question, how does your company support employees who are having life events?

We found out we needed to do better.

One City United is a relationship-based organization. We run in an organized manner and teach that *trust* is the basis of all good relationships. To have trust as the foundation, it must be a two-way street.

It takes individuals being real and vulnerable with one another. It takes the employee and the employer being willing to be vulnerable with one another as to what they know and understand, as well as what they do not know and understand. When working with individuals who have had significant barriers to employment, trust can be a difficult and challenging feat to accomplish.

We have changed policies to reflect our processes for the future. As a small non-profit, we have the liberty to quickly generate changes in policy. However, we know in larger companies those changes may require a bit more of a process.

Please hear me, this is not an excuse to do nothing. Look at your policies today, before you are forced to do it later.

We recently had one of the most difficult terms we have had at One City United. It was a term of pain and heartache because so many individuals in it had significant trauma in their lives. Participants had been shot, seen a parent murdered, were recently released from prison, had lost a limb, were facing eviction, many were in recovery, and most had started their path to healing while in Momentum.

When Momentum is over it is important individuals continue to receive support. To that end, we started a Peer Support Group, because life does not stop happening. We have since expanded it, growing that service within One City's Momentum and beyond within employment. Supporting our staff is an integrated health method proven effective.

Related to health and wellness programs the CDC advises that companies:

- "Evaluate workplace norms and drinking rituals that support substance use. While after-work drinks can help co-workers unwind and make friends, they can undermine the recovery of co-workers. Recovering co-workers may want to avoid alcohol use but might experience social exclusion at work for not participating."
- Focus on the future workforce, "Roughly 90% of individuals with severe substance use disorders began using before the age of 18. Workplaces that employ adolescents and focus on relevant prevention efforts may avoid problems for the next generation of workers." *(CDC)*

What we do in Momentum reminds me of Brene' Brown's use of the words "bad asses" and "bad assery." Individuals work hard to change and really reckon with their past. We have a term that is very real because we all have perceived barriers to overcome. The term is used to describe shattering those perceived barriers, like the glass ceiling for women. If you are offended by an occasional *F bomb* do not insert it. Some people have a tendency to insert the *F bomb* for effect. What we do in a nutshell at One City is to help people get unstuck. "What we do in Momentum is Unstuck People's Mind Stuckery." You can quote me on that.

> 66 It is vital that the dignity and respect of each individual is honored and that ending the stigmas that follow people into the workplaces are handled with bad assery.

Most people have their own pain to process. At One City's Momentum we connect people right away to valuable resources in our community such as counselors, CDAC's, and professionals supporting survivors of domestic violence or sex crimes. Our curriculum naturally starts to uncover some of the root cause of their pain, sometimes adverse childhood experiences. This helps our participants to process and work through it related to employment gaps and how they can get unstuck, by truly knowing their worth. Participants really do have to *trust the process* in turning pain into purpose.

Brene' Brown is much more eloquent than me. In 2015 she shared on Facebook that we really have a badass deficit. Brown recognizes bad assery as, "When I see people stand fully in their truth, or when I see someone fall down, get back up, and say, "Damn. That really hurt, but this is important to me and I'm going in again"—my gut reaction is, "What a badass." These powerful individuals were able to acknowledge their own pain and emulate bad assery. The thing they did not realize is that life continues for all of us, and choosing bad assery through the pain is a constant process. *(Brown)*

It is vital that the dignity and respect of each individual is honored and that ending the stigmas that follow people into the workplaces are handled with bad assery. Staffing situations we face in employment are usually never comfortable. When vulnerability is looked upon as a strength instead of a weakness, that is bad assery. When we listen to understand instead of talking to be understood, that is bad assery. How do you handle adversity? Integrating- to make whole, editing, rewriting and creating new stories.

Change is not easy on anybody, but it's worth it!

Happiness is when what you think, what you say, and what you do are in harmony.

~ Mahatma Gandhi

UnityPoint Health became partners after One City's Executive Director, Dean Feltes, met with Kingsley Botchway who heads up the Human Resource Department. Kingsley took the time to visit Momentum and speak to the participants. When UnityPoint agreed to attend a mock interviewing day Jennifer Oliver walked in the door. She looked around and exclaimed "It came to fruition." She looked at me and asked, with a bewildered look on her face, "You don't recognize me, do you?"

Then I realized it was Jennifer, who I attended college with, and we both joined and served the Phi Theta Kappa service sorority. I was researching and developing this non-profit the entire time we were in college together. Jenni spent time interviewing each participant that first day. Then she showed up the following day for the reverse career fair with a team leader.

At a recent reverse career fair two recruiters, Jenni, from UnityPoint, and Jordan, from the University of Northern Iowa were standing by each other waiting to speak to the potential new hires. I looked at both, and said, "You both hired someone last term!" With a competitive glint in their eyes and sly grins on their faces, they exchanged sidelong glances as they observed the Momentum students. I thought to myself, "This is really cool!" because I just love it when organizational leaders see how people can excel when given the opportunity to grow and thrive. Then, in turn they enhance their own people-first cultures by hiring Momentum graduates.

CHAPTER EIGHT
UnityPoint Health - Waterloo

When Momentum's Luis Sanders interviewed for an environmental services role at UnityPoint Health – Allen Hospital, hiring manager Tim Devine ended the conversation with one final question:

Do you believe in yourself?

The question came after the interview had concluded and the two were exiting the hospital on a mid-summer day.

"That blew me away," Luis said. "I told my girl when I got in the car – he asked me if I believed in myself."

At the time,the Momentum graduate felt he needed to play it cool. He didn't want to seem overconfident or full of himself, so he downplayed the question in the moment, and answered as diplomatically as he could. He thanked Devine for the opportunity before departing.

The truth is, Devine wouldn't have asked the question if he didn't already have a good idea of the real answer.

"Absolutely, positively," Luis will say today.

Sit down with Sanders for a conversation and you might hear him talk more about belief. He had applied for the exact same environmental services role several years ago, but he did not get the job. So there was reason to doubt why it would work out this time.

The difference now may be his completion of the Momentum Program, which Allen Hospital has identified and utilized to fill critical staffing vacancies.

WORKFORCE CHALLENGES

A few years removed from the height of the COVID-19 pandemic that changed healthcare as everyone knew it, Allen Hospital is busier than it has ever been in its nearly 100-year history.

It's difficult to give one singular reason for that. Some will say individuals delayed care amid recommendations to stay home and quarantine, so chronic conditions became worse. There's also an argument that the aging population of Baby Boomers is stressing healthcare resources.

The result at Allen Hospital is a total number of patients from 160 up to 190 on a given day. Not only are there several moving parts when it comes to bedside care performed by physicians, nurses, and other specialists; patients are being discharged quicker and spending less time in the hospital. This is due to the enhancement of home care capability, stronger relationships with assisted living facilities, and better access to outpatient services overall.

It ultimately equals better outcomes for patients. But for Devine and his environmental services team, it means more patient rooms to turn over and an intense focus on working efficiently and diligently to make room for the next individual who requires timely medical care.

Changing linens, disinfecting surfaces, and sanitizing restroom facilities is a broad overview of the responsibilities charged to team members like Sanders.

Devine says it's a near constant to have open positions on his team he's actively looking to fill. Sometimes it's four or five.

"A lot of times, we hire someone who's looking for a change, and they get here for two weeks but realize it's not the change they wanted," he said.

One aspect of Momentum is reinforcing the benefits of growing within oneself along with your occupation. As some have explained, moving from job to job is a good way to continue living paycheck to paycheck.

Nearly six months into working as a patient safety technician, Momentum graduate, Jason York also recognizes the critical role he plays on the overall team. Violent and abusive behavior is often an overlooked aspect of a healthcare professional's day-to-day life. Once again, research has indicated the pandemic increased the severity and frequency of safety events in the hospital due to a higher understanding of illness and a deterioration of mental health among the community at large.

York responds to security calls, primarily in the mental health unit, and works to de-escalate situations using numerous techniques and tactics that continue to evolve. It can be challenging, but that can be said for almost any job. Being recognized and appreciated for making a difference sometimes makes things feel different.

"It is tough some days," he said. "But I do feel accomplished that I'm able to help."

A CAREER THAT MATTERS

Before meeting with recruiter Jenni Oliver, York had never heard of a patient safety tech. He didn't know what it was, but it sounded interesting enough – and working in a hospital was another reason to take a chance.

Now he's reflecting on what his work means and the impact he can have on others.

"I wanted to have a job where I'm actually helping people, making people feel safe, and connecting with people in that way," he said. "It's easy to find a close bond and relationship here."

Oliver first met Jason York at a reverse job fair, where she connected with several Momentum graduates. York stood out for reasons that were surprisingly easy to explain. Oliver never really knew what to expect at events like these, but she did know the kind of person who could be successful.

"His personality was such a great match for that type of role and helping people in those types of challenging situations filled his bucket," Oliver recalls about the hiring decision.

Jason is now thinking about what might be next and ways he can continue to help others. People tell them they feel enlightened or motivated when speaking to him.

Working with the behavioral health population is a draw, and he's considering ongoing education to become a licensed counselor.

Similarly, Pamela Edwards came to Allen Hospital as a referral by Luis Sanders and joined the environmental services team as well. Pamela has prior management experience, a technical training diploma and previously spent time caring for adults with disabilities.

However, criminal history and time served in a correctional facility pushed her to hit the reset button. Back on her feet, Pamela is already asking questions about opportunities for advancement.

"I was in a facility, but I'm not anymore, so for people to believe in us and give us a chance is important," Edwards said.

Again, it was Devine who made a connection during the initial meeting. That conversation sparked something inside Pamela Edwards to not only want to help others, but to want more for herself.

ALIGNMENT WITH MOMENTUM

Details of each team member's story vary, however there is a common theme – something caught their eye that made them think. For some people, a flyer at the grocery store caught their attention, presenting an opportunity to break free from socioeconomic challenges like generational poverty, living paycheck-to-paycheck, and educational disparities.

The end result sounded just fine, but Momentum Luis Sanders isn't afraid to say he had major questions about the path and the process to get there. While everyone was telling him to take a leap of faith, he couldn't make it make sense.

Ultimately, he decided to give it a shot. However, a lack of commitment resulted in missing a day of class. Then he missed another day. And he was out.

"At first I was like – fine," he said. "But I thought about it for a couple of minutes and called back to see what I could do. They saw something in me that I didn't even see in myself, to be honest."

Luis went on to say that several people have since stood up for him. It culminated with his interview and that moment of connection when Devine asked if he believed in himself.

The curriculum of the Momentum Program doesn't delve much into specific job and technical skills. It's career training. It's assessing strengths and weaknesses. It promotes an attitude of personal growth and accountability.

> " " "At first I was like – fine," he said. "But I thought about it for a couple of minutes and called back to see what I could do. They saw something in me that I didn't even see in myself, to be honest."

So, when he thinks back to when he wasn't hired for the same position years ago, he shared his thoughts on his application this time around:

"First thing I said when I applied – they ain't going to hire me."

Devine saw things differently.

"You can definitely tell a difference compared to others who just put on their resume that they're looking for a job," he said. "You can tell that they've got guidance on how to approach an employer and how to make a good first impression."

In addition to seeing benefits related to workforce fulfillment and accommodating a steadily growing demand for healthcare services, UnityPoint Health also aims to be fully representative of its community.

Diversity, equity, and inclusion standards are in place to sustain that growth and best represent the population being served.

"Momentum focuses on underrepresented populations in the Waterloo area," said Kingsley Botchway, director of human resources. "Partnering with this program supports a greater level of exposure to ensure that our team members match the community we serve."

At Allen Hospital, Nick Rosauer oversees the behavioral health programs, including the mental health walk-in clinic. This clinic provides accessible services for individuals experiencing crises who require counseling or medication assistance.

His expertise is amplified through the Momentum program by having him lead a session primarily covering teamwork, barriers to a cohesive work environment, and how to navigate difficult situations.

Rosauer's perspective from each side of the equation – as an employer and as a contributor to the Momentum program – has created an appreciation for certain intangible details. Ultimately it comes down to providing tools and resources that enable everyone to achieve more.

"Many of these skills are often overlooked or have limited opportunities to put into practice before starting a full-time job," Rosauer said. "The program allows and even mandates building these skills through volunteer work. Being great at the basics helps build a foundation to fall back on during the most difficult times of employment and create the best chance of success."

SUSTAINING AN INCLUSIVE WORKPLACE

The decision to provide Momentum graduates with a fresh start and overlook potential past issues aligned with UnityPoint Health's core values and diversity, equity, and inclusion (DEI) initiatives. The organization recognized the importance of addressing barriers and offering opportunities to individuals from diverse backgrounds.

Specifically, the company's FOCUS values stand for: Foster unity, Own the moment, Champion excellence, and Seize opportunities.

During annual performance reviews, every team member, including human resources personnel who screen potential candidates and senior leaders responsible for driving the organization forward, is evaluated based on their adherence to those core values.

The values must be considered more than words in the employee handbook by everyone making decisions.

"When you talk about establishing a strong culture, it often takes intentional decision-making and action to support that. It's not something that just happens," said Botchway. "If you do it right, the result is a culture that elevates everyone's feeling of belonging."

In other words, recognizing that everyone is different is the first step. Understanding how those differences create benefits is where transformation begins. This may become difficult when everyone agrees on an end goal – sharing the vision of a good outcome is easy – but there is unspoken skepticism when it comes down to the steps needed to get there.

Allen Hospital has also had success providing internship opportunities through Project SEARCH – a program designed to give life-skill education and employment opportunities to youth with developmental disabilities. For team members working with SEARCH interns for the first time, it can be uncomfortable or difficult to adjust to different styles of learning and sharing the same intellectual space.

But the truth is, that may be the case in any new interaction – even when another person looks, sounds, and acts just like you. In a just culture, everyone learns how to work alongside one another, and differences become nothing more than a first impression.

"We've been able to reinforce a culture of inclusion through transparent communication," Botchway added. "We listen to our team members' feedback through engagement surveys and in-person rounding. When there are concerns, we want to explore that whenever possible and use our values as a guide to work through it."

 We've been able to reinforce a culture of inclusion through transparent communication," Botchway added.

Brick-and-mortar examples include a fitness facility and a day care center opening in the past two years near the Allen Hospital campus. UnityPoint Health took on the financial burden of these startups as an additional way to show team members that their concerns matter and fulfill specific requests to create a culture that allows individuals to be themselves.

ONE can do a great deal of good in this world if one doesn't care who gets the credit for it.

~ The Friend - Father Strickland,
English Jesuit

Western Home Communities has a creative and innovative educational model that initiates educational opportunities for future healthcare employees. One City United's leadership recently spoke at a conference for the Western Home Communities Directors Meeting. We were able to thank them for investing in the life of one of our graduates.

This graduate shared that during her term, she really felt she was to give back and serve others. I recommended that she attend the University of Iowa's Peer Support Specialist program.

This graduate also decided to enroll in Western Homes Certified Nurse's Aide Apprenticeship. She was given the opportunity to begin a position in what she had previously thought would be her dream job. Then her faith and relationship with God led her in a different direction. She had completed an in-person education with Western Home Communities that added to her passion and purposeful goal of becoming a counselor.

I thanked Western Home Communities for being the launching pad for this individual, so she could start believing in herself, and her educational aspirations. She enrolled in college to pursue a career in counseling and took a part-time position, using her peer support specialist certification, working with others in recovery. We are deeply grateful to Western Home Communities for generously providing an opportunity that did not directly benefit them, displaying gratitude for their gracious and selfless action.

The Hospitality Coordinator, Randall Carlson, started an Advanced Leadership class at One City United. We have an attitude of gratitude for Western Home Communities and their heart for community development.

CHAPTER NINE
· Western Home Communities

Something to ponder: Would your business include employees in its mission statement?

Western Home Communities, a charitable Christian service organization, answered with a resounding YES! They have enthusiastically supported the Momentum program. This partnership aligned perfectly with their mission of creating fulfilling lifestyles for residents, families, and employees. They viewed employee contributions to such initiatives as mission-critical to their organization.

"We take care of people here, whether it's providing social outlets for active living or the assistance that's needed to get through the day," says Kris Hansen, CEO of the aging services provider, based in Cedar Falls. "If we don't take care of employees well, how can they take care of everyone who's depending on us?"

 "Even before COVID-19, the healthcare worker shortage forced us to be more intentional and solution-oriented regarding hiring and retention," Hansen explains.

Understanding that perspective, it's easy to see how Western Home Communities has long embraced outside-the-box thinking regarding workforce development.

Recent organizational growth, coupled with unprecedented external challenges, brought employment to the forefront, making it an organization-wide focus instead of the sole concern of human resources.

"Even before COVID-19, the healthcare worker shortage forced us to be more intentional and solution-oriented regarding hiring and retention," Hansen explains. "Then the need exponentiated during the pandemic. A lot of the demographic we typically hire from decided to leave the workforce, at least temporarily. We needed to get creative across the board – who we hired, how we hired and trained, how we scheduled caregivers, and more."

Western Home Communities responded with an all-hands-on-deck approach. Leaders understood that the quality of care was in jeopardy, which meant the sustainability of the organization was at risk.

They knew old approaches wouldn't work, and repeating the same strategies, while expecting different results would be pointless. So they started a new approach by thoughtfully listening and responding to what employees told them would be helpful.

In addition to raising wages, the organization created "option pay," a higher hourly rate in lieu of benefits, as another way to provide flexibility. It works well for employees working fewer hours or who may have benefits through a spouse's workplace.

Employee recognition became a regular feature on social media. Retention bonuses helped reward employees who have longer tenures. Well-defined career lattices helped keep others on board who wanted to work toward advancement; those employees can also take advantage of tuition reimbursement policies and employee scholarships as they pursue more education.

Additional training and development opportunities were offered, including an in-house leadership development curriculum. The clinical team established a "Learn & Earn Center" to offer additional onboarding for its new employees and ongoing training.

The organization started an apprenticeship program with funding provided by Iowa Workforce Development.

Western Home Communities partnered with Cedar Falls Center for Advanced Professional Studies (CAPS) and the Waterloo Career Center to train high school students as CNAs; those who are out of high school can apply for the in-house CNA class. This allows students to be paid while learning and have a job at Western Home Communities when they're certified.

The organization recruited dozens of hospitality workers from Jamaica who wanted to add American work experience to their credentials. The year-long cultural exchange, under the auspices of the State Department's J-1 Visa program, introduced residents and co-workers alike to customs and cuisines that quickly became new favorites.

Employee mental health became more of a focus as the heightened stress and forced isolation brought on by the pandemic took an emotional toll. The Employee Assistance Program, which had been in place for years, became more heavily promoted. Additional mental health information was offered to employees via the intranet and at daily team huddle meetings.

Western Home Communities' steps involved multiple departments, high-level leaders, effective communication, and timely action.

It wasn't easy, even though the organization has "People First" as a core value, because the external forces created so much pressure. Hansen says the organization passed the test. "Putting a greater intentionality behind it, while becoming nimbler and more solution-oriented, has paid off dramatically," Hansen says.

Hanson went on to say, "The situation challenged us to better understand our needs in this environment and prepare for the future. As a result, we've successfully grown our workforce and we've all learned a lot along the way."

As all these efforts were being developed and implemented, Hansen attended a Diversity, Equity and Inclusion Summit where, he learned of One City's Momentum Urban Employment Initiative. He reached out to learn more and see how it would fit with the organization. Since another core value for Western Home Communities is innovation, Hansen regularly looks for unique opportunities, especially those that involve community collaboration.

> On their first day of orientation, new employees learn how they can and should play a role in living out the four core values – People First, Servant Spirit, Innovation, and Financial Integrity.

"I believe in what One City wants to do with ex-offenders and others who have barriers to employment. One City works to get them through these tough challenges by mentoring and training. It's life-changing for many of them, and that creates a win-win situation."

That core value of innovation means change is a constant within the organization – not for the sake of change itself, but to realize the mission of assertively creating fulfilling lifestyles.

"There are thousands of people in several Iowa communities who depend on us to lead the way and make their lives better," Hansen explains. "That can be new technology, new services, or new ways of doing things. Even if that means upsetting the apple cart a bit, we always want to keep being better."

On their first day of orientation, new employees learn how they can and should play a role in living out the four core values – People First, Servant Spirit, Innovation, and Financial Integrity. Putting the values into practice is a constant focus and helps build a strong workplace culture.

Telling that story has helped pique the interest of those who might not have thought of healthcare and aging services as a dynamic career field.

"Western Home Communities has always been inclusive in our hiring; what had to change was being creative and getting the word out," explains Talent Acquisition Specialist Alex Covarrubias. "One City has helped us get in front of a candidate pool we might not have reached before," he went on to say.

In Covarrubias's experience, many potential candidates worry that they won't be hired for a healthcare position because of their background, which she says, is not the case.

"Our process allows for unbiased opportunity. Essentially, if you have a great resume and interview, you're a qualified candidate," she explains. "That's why we're grateful to One City for helping people learn how to put together an effective resume and prepare for interview questions."

She believes investing in future employees and creating opportunities for all individuals has created an even more inclusive environment within the organization.

The positive results prove that an organization over a century old can successfully adapt and change with the times to survive.

Western Home Communities started in 1912 as a home for aged church members of the Evangelical Association, a mostly German denomination that later became part of the United Methodist Church. The organization expanded to a second campus in Cedar Falls in the early 1990s, and then accelerated its growth in 2000.

Since then, it has built nearly 300 villas for active living and upended its nursing home model to provide privacy, dignity, and purpose for the frailest residents. The organization built new cottages or renovated existing buildings to create small homes instead of hospital-like institutions.

 The positive results prove that an organization over a century old can successfully adapt and change with the times to survive.

This innovative household model of care throws out the old model that functioned around staff schedules instead of resident desires. Residents now get to choose their preferred daily rhythms, and every single person enjoys a private spacious suite with an attached bathroom.

In 2018, Western Home Communities opened the lifestyle hub of Jorgensen Plaza, featuring a wellness and aquatic center, physical therapy center, event space for 400, salon spa, unique gift shop, and a pub that earns rave reviews for its food and cocktails. These amenities are open to the public and are in demand by a population that wants to focus on all aspects of well-being as they age.

The youngest of the Baby Boomer generation turns 60 in 2024, so their demand for aging services will keep the sector vibrant for years to come. Career opportunities will continue to grow, even outside of the

Cedar Valley; Western Home Communities now manages or owns other senior living communities in Grundy Center, Jesup, Ackley, Reinbeck, and Madrid. They are planning new developments in Waterloo, Iowa City, and Cedar Rapids.

That means the organization will keep fine-tuning its recruiting strategies and continue partnering with One City to find new employees eager to embrace the opportunity. Hansen says that any company, new or old, in any line of work, can benefit from seeing people for their potential, instead of their past.

"I think it's just being open-minded and seeing what barriers you truly have, versus simply the perceptions you may have," he advises. "In the beginning, ask 'why not?' then change your mindset and GO!"

The meaning of life is to find your gift.
The purpose of life is to give it away.

~ Pablo Picasso

CHAPTER TEN

Seeing Lives Changed!

WHAT WE DID, WHY WE DID IT, SEEING LIVES CHANGED!

As I reflect on serving the community, what fires me up is not an achievement or an accomplishment for One City United, it's what those graduates are doing by making real life changes. Though I should mention a recent award because it really surprised us, but again it is because of those making the real-life changes. One City United was chosen for the Exceptional Nonprofit of the Year for 2024. That was a great surprise that the Northeast Iowa Community Foundation nominated us for through the University of Northern Iowa's Nonprofit Alliance.

What really lights a fire within my soul is seeing lives radically being transformed through mindsets changing, people being willing to learn and listen to others, and hear different points of view. When people can change their minds, their viewpoint changes.

What they once saw as a failure or mistake becomes a learning experience on the path to their purpose. I get to be the recipient of the joy their accomplishments give. God sends me back to remedial school every time my own perspective gets off base. I know it's the same for some others. When people take their newfound knowledge and apply it, I appreciate every challenging day and every struggle it has taken in this journey. My biggest accolade is getting to be a witness and see passion meeting purpose in an individual's life. That it is so very rewarding. Community development happens when we see leaders rise from within to seek solutions to problems within our community. That really lights my fire!

Even though Dean and I grew up with very little diversity, our parents truly loved mankind. They were (mine) and are (Dean's) exceptionally good human beings. I remember my mother using her nursing education, caring for people, and being a visiting nurse before it was an actual career path. I would see the smiles she would leave in her path as she helped others. My father loved his dairy farm, and his herd of registered Holstein cows. He enjoyed being involved through his alma mater, Iowa State University, engaging in innovative crop farming practices that are now commonly used today. His farm was one of the first to use terraces.

My parents thought outside of the box. They were both strong believers and followers of Jesus Christ. I grew up in a holy roller Methodist Church. I didn't really know it or understand it until I was an adult. Faith was a huge part of my life growing up. My parents had strong aspirations for their children.

The Feltes family is a loving, strong German Catholic family. Dean told me early in our marriage, "You know you are loved without words needing to be said." They are a tight-knit and a rock-solid family. We recently shared we didn't know how good we had it growing up until in ministry, hearing the stories of people who have struggled. Every challenge we have had since has been a life lesson to prepare us for future life lessons.

LIVES BEING TRANSFORMED

Pedro came to Momentum a little over a year ago while living in the Salvation Army Men's Shelter. He was homeless. I made him jump through some hoops to even be considered for class. Prior to Pedro coming to One City United, the last homeless gentleman to graduate relapsed immediately after graduation and it tore me up. That is when I decided that I would challenge Pedro to follow through with getting connected to the resources he needed prior to being admitted to

Momentum. I asked him to connect with a local community behavioral health clinic to check into the services offered. I knew he would need part-time employment to live and eventually move from the shelter. He followed through. Once admitted into Momentum, Pedro didn't miss a day of class. He had some life challenges while in class. I was unaware of how he had been hurt by church people. Pedro intentionally did not share he had a criminal background when he heard Dean had been a pastor and I had been a youth leader. This was out of fear of being ostracized once again.

It was not until after Pedro graduated, he had some challenges with his mental health, he reached out for help, I then realized he was like an onion that has many layers and he was ready to start peeling them away. I didn't fully know of Pedro's background because he intentionally did not share. We were "church people" and not one but two local churches had hurt him deeply. He had served time due to some things he had done as a teenager. Pedro's first challenge was that he was raised by a father who treated him terribly. Then the second was he lived the life expected of him. What we were teaching was a new normal. Pedro needed to focus on his wholeness. He needed to lose the toxic relationship he was in and continue to invest in himself.

The day he called in the depths of depression, I was not the first call he made. Pedro called 911 and asked the 911 dispatcher to call me because he was unsure if he wanted to live or die that day. The 911 operator called me and asked "Where does Pedro live?" I was driving and could only give general directions. 911 followed up by calling the emergency mobile crisis unit. The social worker who rides along with the police works for the same community behavioral health clinic I had Pedro connect to before I would allow him into Momentum. I called my pastor and asked him to pray without giving specific information.

I witnessed an innovative intervention that our local police and mental health providers are now using. The ride-along social worker went in before the police. It was not long until Pedro walked out.

Pedro's girlfriend at the time showed up on the scene and it only took me a minute to realize she had some challenges herself and needed to be in recovery. Pedro walked out, gave me a hug and got into the police car with the mobile crisis unit. I later called the hospital and asked Pedro if I could visit him. I visited and so did my pastor. Pedro had been so deeply hurt throughout his life by rejections. That day he had planned to throw a toaster in the tub and electrocute himself. Fortunately, he could not find an extension cord long enough.

Pedro decided to again trust "church people" and started to attend Evansdale Church of the Nazarene. Pedro found a much needed healthy church community there. A church community without stigmas around mental health, recovery and re-entry. It was not until Pedro was baptized that I heard about the many times he had been rejected throughout his life. He was way too scared to share his background with me because of the deep seated pain it caused him.

Pedro had to change things before things could change. He had already been employed and gotten housing. But, when Pedro started focusing on his goals related to the dimensions of wellness which included his relationships, his health, and spirituality, things started to change for the better. I encouraged him to apply for a multilingual human resource position at a manufacturing corporation. He had the skills needed and I knew he would be an excellent fit. Since taking all these steps Pedro is now in a position where he recruits Momentum graduates. He likes to come into classes early in the six weeks, usually to teach a class, and then again later at the career fair.

Pedro proposed to the love of his life at church on Christmas Eve. Pedro sent his fiance', Victoria, to Momentum because he knew it would change her life for the better and she too could find her passion and purpose. Pedro's journey is an example of what fills my bucket with joy!

OPPORTUNITIES ARE WHERE PASSION MEETS PURPOSE

One City's Momentum is half social services and half employment. Our focus on career development involves exploration and discovery with each individual. We want to meet the desires of each person's heart where passion meets their purpose.

Henry was the first Bosnian immigrant to attend Momentum. Henry lived at home with his parents, he held a good paying job, faced some mental health challenges that caused him much concern, so much so that he needed to leave a very stressful governmental position. His family did not understand why he would seek out a program that served so many individuals in recovery and with criminal backgrounds. It confused them and probably caused them some concern. They immigrated to the United States to give their family a better life and then their son decides to attend a program with people who have had legal challenges.

Henry recently told a Momentum class his story. He shared what his family told him, "You don't have the same types of problems everyone else does, you're not a drug addict, you're not homeless, you don't have a background. They tried to classify everyone else as different. You don't have the same types of problems, but when I first started here, I realized everyone has the same struggles." To move forward Henry had to stop listening to those around him who were holding him back. Henry thoroughly checked out the Momentum program by attending the previous graduation to hear other graduates' stories. He did exactly what any person with a DISC personality of a high C would do, research, analyze, and heavily vet this program for its worthiness of his time. DISC is a personality assessment that helps people to understand themselves and understand those around them.

We find during the entire Momentum program, listening to understand is the key. We listen so we can mine for gold in those who are investing six weeks of their life to learn and self-explore.

In Henry's case he invested wisely. He set his goals, looked at his opportunities, and applied for jobs that were in his skill set. Henry didn't stop there though because he had a deep desire to advance on his education.

When I learned Henry wanted to become an EMT Emergency Management Technician I started making contacts with him. In the meantime, Henry received six job offers. That really caused him additional concerns because he really wanted to attend college but knew he'd need a job. We weighed the pros and cons of each, and he decided to take a position with a local hospital as an operating room supply technician. I thought to myself, "what a great position for an individual who is extremely concise and correct!" The hospital worked with Henry on adjusting his schedule around college.

He recently graduated as an EMT from our local community college. His next step in achieving his career aspirations is becoming a paramedic. He transferred to the ambulance crew and is doing just that at Hawkeye Community College. I have no doubt in my mind he will do it! One City Momentum works!

CJ: SORROW TO SEEING A BRIGHTER TOMORROW

Momentum is designed to emulate work. We require 100 hours of volunteering by each participant to graduate, in addition to the 3.5 hours of classroom time they experience every day for six intense weeks.

When CJ enrolled in Momentum, he had recently lost his mother to a stroke. He found Momentum through a flier at our local People's Clinic. CJ was 24 years old and the youngest man to enroll in Momentum, at that time. While in class he volunteered for a newly emerging youth program, designed to keep youth and kids in crisis from entering the criminal justice system. I fell in love with the concept because we had worked with kids in the ATEV program and taken kids into our home with similar challenges.

I met Brittany, the director, prior to the county opening the Brownstone program. She came to One City and visited with a couple of our Momentum participants. CJ immediately shared his interest in working with kids. Brittany offered CJ some volunteer time painting and assisting in preparation for the youth organization to open up. He jumped right on it and showed off his work ethic.

Prior to graduating Momentum CJ participated in a Reverse Career Fair where the script is flipped, and the Human Resource professionals seek out the participants. This event has been very successful in starting our graduates into their careers. Both of our local hospitals, as well as other healthcare, production, fulfillment, and manufacturing companies, have hired multiple Momentum graduates.

After the event, CJ had a second interview at the hospital. I took him and he seemed anxious before going in. He shared the last time he had walked through the doors of the hospital was the last time he saw his mother alive.

CJ was offered and accepted a position at a hospital as a surgical technician. While CJ was interviewing, I managed to pick up something at the hospital gift shop. It was a stone that had the inscription "Mom" on it. I figured CJ could carry it in his pocket and it would remind him to think of his mom as his rock. And so he could know how proud she would be of every accomplishment he makes in his life. I have carried similar items that would remind me to pray for a family member.

The orientation for the surgery tech position is pretty intense and takes months to complete. CJ had been in this position for 30 days when Brittany reached out with an opportunity to work for the Department of Corrections.

The absolute irony is CJ was on probation himself, at that time, and would be working with youth on probation. I believe this is what needs to happen to lower recidivism and promote reform. CJ had received a DUI (Driving Under the Influence) after trying to drown his sorrows away with alcohol after his mother died. This is the reason for his probation.

His mother raised him to be a kind and respectful young man, and it was no surprise that the Department of Corrections recognized his potential. I believe that this gentle giant, with such a calming demeanor, would definitely impact lives by living out who he is, and sharing his change with teens headed the wrong way.

It seems everyone who meets CJ cannot help themselves and must inquire, "Do you play basketball?" At 6 ft 6 inches, CJ has a strong yet caring personality. The youth in our detention center need someone to head them down the right path. Just this month CJ was released from probation. As an employment professional, I believe it is a perfect career choice for CJ!

TRUST THE PROCESS

Matthew was in an early term of Momentum. I met him on day two, when I taught the career exploration class. The next time I went to teach class that week he wasn't there. He had received a violation from his Probation Officer and was sent back to jail. I'd given everyone my business card and the following Saturday my phone started blowing up! One call after another, one family member after another. Men in the jail started calling me inquiring about this program called Momentum.

I spent the entire evening fielding calls and answering questions. This was all because of Matthew. He was sharing what he had been learning in the first three days of One City's Momentum classes with the other inmates in his pod, at the jail.

The men started sharing the information with their families. Matthew had shared the hope we had started to instill in him with others. "This program is going to change my life!" It was the family members calling me!

Then I received a call from the jail social workers wanting to know what One City was doing in this program called Momentum. Matthew came out two terms later, on the third day of class.

The first two weeks engage participants in teaching hope, then the next two weeks become more intense focusing on change, which is a transformational pedagogy, meaning the method of how teachers teach, in theory and in practice. It is very structured.

Then we introduce Opportunity. Matthew embraced the program to the fullest. When he came with his employer to share his story with other Momentum students, he said, "Trust the Process!"

Matthew knows what Momentum education did for him. It better equipped him to effectively communicate in challenging situations. Matthew became an excellent employee, father, and friend to his son's mother. He went from hardly seeing his child to fully embracing fatherhood and raising him.

In the Momentum program, we teach participants they no longer must be pawns controlled by others. Instead, they have the potential to live a life of empowerment and fulfillment, akin to a king, if they trust and commit to the transformative process, which can be challenging but ultimately leads to a profound life transformation. One City's Momentum works!

PEER SUPPORT GROWS OUR WORKFORCE

Mickie came to Momentum on the referral of several people from her church and her family. She had worked for a local manufacturer and made pretty good money. However, she knew that wasn't the path she was supposed to take. Mickie was in recovery from alcohol and is a single mom. As I listened to her share her interest in assisting others in their recovery, it only seemed natural that obtaining a Peer Support Recovery Specialist certification should be on that path. Mickie was excited about it when I shared this new integrated health career. We researched it further together and Mickie enrolled in the University of Iowa's Workforce Collaborative. Opportunities seem to unfold in multiple ways, because our participants are ready to begin a career path. Mickie really wanted to go into healthcare. She also enrolled in the Western Home Communities certified nurse's aide education. Mickie dove fully into expanding her educational opportunities. She really enjoyed the peer recovery specialist education.

While in Momentum, Mickie became very interested in the safety technician position at UnityPoint Hospital. After Momentum, her determination showed through multiple employment opportunities all at once at Western Home Communities and UnityPoint Health Hospital!

Then Mickie called and asked to meet. She wanted to discuss how her faith was getting in the way of her plans. We attended Mickie's recent baptism. She was really listening to the Holy Spirit for guidance. She shared, "God is changing everything up." She told us, "Right when I think I know everything I want to do, God changed my direction."

As believers, a former youth leader and pastor, we are very familiar with how God redirects and changes the course for people unexpectedly. We were happy for Mickie when she announced she had been offered a position at a local recovery and behavioral health center in their inpatient treatment center. Then she shared that she now realized that she needed to go to college to become a recovery counselor.

The education Western Homes poured into Mickie was not lost. It was the community's gain. Mickie is working in her values, embracing the dimensions of wellness and has since completed her first year of college. She loves her job and enjoys assisting others in their recovery. Mickie has been doing some of her internship as a peer support specialist with One City United's Momentum program. One City's Momentum works!

HUMAN CAPITAL- EMPLOYMENT SOLUTIONS

Recognizing the need for change in organizational processes is not an instant solution for staff retention, shifting long-held mindsets, and becoming a people-first culture workplace. To truly rehumanize employment, companies and organizations must refrain from marginalizing candidates based on their past mistakes or worst moments in life. Instead, they should embrace a more inclusive approach that considers the whole person, not just their previous experiences.

To embrace becoming people-first workplaces, companies must take the time to understand and learn from experienced professionals who have committed to challenging the status quo. This is what we do at One City United.

People-First Employers embrace resistance as a natural part of change and learn from pre-existing mindsets that are based on perceptions, perspectives, prejudices, and biases. We all have them and should focus on the dimensions of wellness to better understand that we need to address them. Perceptions, perspectives, prejudices, and biases are not dirty or shameful words. The only shameful thing is when we, as a society, are not willing to embrace and understand the emotional intelligence it takes to process and unpack what these four very important words have meant in our lives.

The questions you may ask:

1. How can my company benefit by truly rehumanizing employment and taking on the long-held stigmas of mental health, recovery, and re-entry?
2. How do we remain professional and not get too personal with our employees, yet be truly People-First?

One City United does challenge the status quo in hiring by teaching, training, and equipping corporate leaders and supervisors while supporting both tenured employees and new hires.

WE BEGIN WITH THE END IN MIND

Phase One: In our work in this area, Dean, our amazing team of collaborators, and I engage with company leaders through innovation. We ask them the thought-provoking question, "What needs to change?" and then identify the specific needs related to company culture, staffing requirements, and retention practices.

We propose solutions that will foster effective change, leading to the development of a cohesive team that embraces and desires a People First Culture. This culture prioritizes the well-being and engagement of both existing tenured staff and newly hired, high-quality employees during the onboarding process.

Phase Two: Dean has excellent discernment skills. He can work with your company to create a culture that will embrace necessary policy and procedure changes while developing the processes that lead to People-First Cultures. As non-profit leaders, we have learned to best understand the early, mid, and late adopters. As a skilled relational router (with the gift of rallying staff), I am able to find core values in the lives of current company employees.

Phase Three: Our team will identify your most tenacious employees who can implement and enable change by bringing these cultural shifts to fruition. Everyone has a role to play in enacting and legitimizing The New Hustle and Create People-First Workplaces that re-humanizes employment, by blending backgrounds and cultures . . . creating Opportunities for All.

When your company creates a New Hustle and People-First Culture, employees' values and needs are met. They will in turn meet your company's mission with gratitude and longevity in your workforce.

Alone we can do so little; together we can do so much.

~ Helen Keller

CHAPTER ELEVEN

Dean on Prejudice

When I was young, I lived inside of this bubble that was very focused on work. I had a hard-working dad who worked a forty-hour-a-week job and committed another thirty hours to the farm.

While my father worked during the day, my mother managed the household. She kept my two brothers, sister, and me disciplined and helped with farm work, when necessary. We all worked together, doing whatever it took daily to keep everything running smoothly and productive.

Growing up on a farm contributed heavily to the way I saw the world, and the way I believed that everyone must think exactly the way I did. That work was something that had to be done, you might enjoy some of it, you might hate most of it, but in the end that didn't really matter. And to be honest, I did enjoy most of the farm life and the work that went along with it, even though most of my days were spent either working or in school.

We worked hard and played hard. We lived a comfortable middle-class lifestyle. We never worried about our next meal and always had more than enough. Our financial stability allowed us to take vacations, own vehicles, and live without constant financial pressure or urgency.

Honestly, I kind of assumed that most everyone lived just like I did.

It wasn't until I graduated high school and started working off of the farm that I discovered not everyone was like me, a small-town hick with a very sheltered view of the world.

I watched the nightly news and read media reports regularly about struggles occurring both nationally and globally. However, I mistakenly assumed these were isolated incidents that didn't affect most people. I was amazed that there were so many different points of view on what I considered seemingly meaningless subjects.

I had no idea there were so many people who had experienced a radically different childhood from mine. To learn that there were people who actually didn't eat meat, only fruits and veggies, seriously rocked my world.

 What I did not realize is that I was living with a foundation of prejudice and bias.

I began to experience people who had very different cultures than the one I was raised in. Even though it was intriguing to me, I wasn't quite ready to open my mind and my heart to believe that people who lived differently than me weren't messed up in the way they were living.

I guess that is what we call prejudice:
- preconceived judgment or opinion
- an adverse opinion or leaning formed without just grounds or before sufficient knowledge

(Merrium Webster Dictionary)

I had never thought of myself as someone who was living with prejudice as my foundation. I wasn't against anyone, I simply believed that my way of thinking, my life experience, my understanding was always right.

How could I possibly be wrong? My world view was serving me very well thank you. In my family, for generations, we have believed and lived according to some pretty basic patterns and unspoken rules, along with some mandates.

How could the way I live and the way I approach life ever be suspect to scrutiny, how could I believe there was more than one approach to life that may be fulfilling for someone else?

What I did not realize is that I was living with a foundation of prejudice and bias. I had unknowingly and unintentionally fallen into the trap that so often catches people, agencies, organizations, and businesses alike.

This trap is insidious, subtle, and so extremely comfortable for all who will place their life within its clutches.

The challenge with prejudice is simple; we don't set out to form an opinion without sufficient knowledge, it happens very slowly over time. Many times, the way we believe, the way we view the world, the way we view people who's lives have been different than ours are formed in ignorance.

Simply put, we don't know what we don't know.

In my opinion, prejudice is neither wrong nor right, it simply "is". It is our cumulative life experiences, our culture, the knowledge we have accumulated, our beliefs (founded or not), and every form of input that has impacted our lives.

Every person that walks the face of the earth lives with prejudice that has been formed through their life to this point. Prejudice in and of itself isn't the issue, it's when we recognize that we have a prejudice that is unjust, misplaced, or simply wrong . . . and we refuse to embrace the revealed truth.

I am a firm believer in gaining knowledge. I love to learn new things at every turn and from any resource that is available. Those who know me well have labeled me the King of FOUI, which is an acronym for "Fountain Of Useless Information."

> After all, ignorance is the foundation that all of my prejudice is built on.

I have never met a fact or statistic that I wasn't interested in understanding at a deeper level, understanding the how and the why. I used to believe that the answer to overcoming all of the world's challenges, inequities, and struggles was knowledge; if everyone would gain more knowledge then change would happen. That makes sense right? The more I can learn about people and their way of life, the better I can understand them. The more knowledge I can gain about different cultures and beliefs, the better I can understand them. With more knowledge, we can create an entirely new world, where we all can edify each other, show compassion to each other, and experience world peace.

As I said, I used to believe that knowledge was the key to unlocking the trap of prejudice and bias. And I do believe that knowledge is the first step, because ignorance definitely is not any part of the solution, in any circumstance.

After all, ignorance is the foundation that all of my prejudice is built on.

Instead, we must have a foundation of knowledge to build this structure of understanding on, or it will certainly fail. If knowledge is the first step, then the second step that we have to take is called experience.

In my opinion and experience, knowledge by itself, without the benefit of real-life experience is in and of itself dangerous. Think of it this way: You go to the hospital with chest pain, and they do all of the tests to find out that you are having a heart attack. They rush you into surgery and the masked man comes into the room and lets you know that he has never done heart surgery before.

But, he has studied all of the text books, has seen the surgery done on multiple videos, and is very confident he can do the double bypass without any trouble at all.

After all, he has all of the knowledge, he's studied for years, everything should be just fine, right?

The question: Are you going to allow this guy, with all of the knowledge and absolutely no experience cut into your chest? Why not?

If knowledge is the key, then this surgery should be performed without any adverse consequences, right?

Just grab a scalpel and let's get this surgery done. Probably not the answer that any one of us would have. We would send this guy packing and get a surgeon who possesses both the knowledge and the experience.

My challenge, your challenge, the challenge that faces us all in this world; To understand that the way I see the world, the way that I understand people who are different than me, is very incomplete.

I only know what I know, I've only experienced the people, circumstances, and situations that I have experienced. So, what is the answer, what is the "way out" of living in my narrow view, allowing prejudice to rule my view of the world and of people?

Experience.

The key to breaking down and removing potentially damaging and hurtful prejudices in my life is to gain knowledge and then to experience new people, new cultures, new places, and new ways of thinking.

One of our greatest assets as a human is that our brains like to create order. It enables us to think strategically and conceptually. It also allows us to plan effectively in many different arenas of life.

However, one of our greatest strengths is also one of our greatest weaknesses. Our brain often imposes order on our lives by categorizing and grouping information into neat, easily understandable compartments.

Just think about something as simple as food; fruits, vegetables, meat, fish, and bread. Then we create subcategories to give even more definition to the category we have created.

The weakness in this approach comes when we start to do the same with people. We start with physical appearance, maybe the amount of pigment in someone's skin, their nation of origin, body type, male or female, physical appearance, and how they dress. Then our brain wants to naturally place this person in one of the categories we've created.

Then, as we actually greet this new person we begin the next evaluation process; how does this person talk, what is their education level, do they seem kind or rude, positive or negative. If we can all be honest, we usually have a person categorized within a minute or less, definitely less if we don't get into a conversation and simply see someone from across the room.

 . . . we dehumanize individuals, simply so they can fit into one of the groups that we have created, so we can more easily live our life in peace.

"People grouping" is the primary cause of nearly all of the racism, bias, terrorism, and negative prejudice we experience in the world. We give these people groups names, titles, and brands along with all of our associated assumptions.

Through this practice we dehumanize individuals, simply so they can fit into one of the groups that we have created, so we can more easily live our life in peace. I won't assume that you have consciously developed these groups, I know I didn't. But I do know this, we all do it, whether consciously or subconsciously.

Several years ago, I experienced a sudden influx of cultural diversity in my life. I began meeting new people weekly whose life experiences were vastly different from my own. People who didn't look like me, people from other countries, who spoke different languages, men and women recovering from addiction, men and women returning from prison, people who were homeless, dozens of differing religious experiences.

I caught myself trying to neatly place each person into a category. However, the new categories were growing by the day, and I couldn't keep up anymore. That was when I realized how destructive and dehumanizing my process of people grouping was.

Each person I met was a unique individual, with different strengths and weaknesses, different dreams, different life experiences, and family experiences. They were all from the same general geographical area of a country that was not the United States of America.

I was blown away! I was ashamed of myself. That day forever changed my life.

Placing people in a group simply for my peace of mind, my ability to be comfortable living inside of my own prejudice or to resist having to make changes in my life, is shameful.

When we strip away the categories, the titles, and the stigmas; what is left?

Human beings.

My final thought is this: When will we simply be human with each other? When will we strip away everything else, and simply see each other as human beings?

When will we simply sit across from each other at a table and be human beings?

Honestly, that is my hope and prayer. I believe it is the only hope that will change our divisive, negative, and polarizing world today. Go out and be human today!

Thank You for Reading
Legitimizing the New Hustle
Please share your thoughts and reactions.

Recommended Reading

Employment

- **Crucial Conversations** by *Patterson, Grenny, McMillan, & Switzler*
- **HELP! I work With People** by *Chad Veach*
- **KPIs A New Approach** by *Robertson Hunter Stewart*
- **The 6 Types of WORKING GENIUS** by *Patrick Lencioni*
- **The FIVE DYSFUNCTIONS of a TEAM** by *Patrick Lencioni*
- **STICKY TEAMS** by *Larry Osborne*
- **SWITCH: How To Change Things When Change Is Hard** by *Chip Heath & Dan Heath*
- **THINKING FOR A CHANGE: 11 Ways Highly Successful People Approach Life and Work** by *John C. Maxwell*

Transformational Understanding

- **Atlas of the Heart** by *Brene' Brown*
- **Caste** by *Isabel Wilkerson*
- **Daring Greatly** by *Brene' Brown*
- **From Prison to Purpose: Redeemed by God's Grace** by *Shane Blackledge*
- **Geography Of Grace** by *Kris Rocke & Joel Van Dyke*
- **Irresistible Revolution** by *Shane Caliborne*
- **Last Lecture** by *Randy Pausch, Jeffrey Zaslow*
- **Let Justice Roll Down** by *John M. Perkins*
- **The New Jim Crow** by *Michelle Alexander*
- **THE TURN: from who we are, to who we were created to be** by *Rusty Boruff*

References & Citations

- "6 Effective Employee Retention Strategies for 2023." Workhuman, 19 Oct. 2023, www.workhuman.com/blog/effective-employee-retention-strategies/.
- "About." Iowa Peer Workforce Collaborative - The University of Iowa, iowapeersupport.sites.uiowa.edu/about. Accessed 3 Sept. 2024.
- Alton, L. (2023, June 5). 5 must-haves for employee retention in 2022. SPARK. https://www.adp.com/spark/articles/2022/03/5-must-haves-for-employee-retention-in-2022.aspx
- Bentley, Stacy. "Ideal Reader Questionnaire." One City United, Aug. 2023.
- Borglum, Chris. "Ideal Reader Questionnaire." One City United, Aug. 2023.
- Botchway, Kingsley. "Ideal Reader Questionnaire." One City United, September 2024.
- Brown, Brene', and Eric Mosley. "Brené with Eric Mosley on Making Work Human." Brené with Eric Mosley on Making Work Human, 17 Jan. 2024, brenebrown.com/podcast/brene-with-eric-mosley-on-making-work-human/.
- Brown, Brene'. "Chapter 12/Dehumanization." Atlas Of The Heart, Mapping Meaningful Connection and the Language of Human Experience, Random House, 2021, pp. 233–235.
- Chapman, Gary D., and Paul E. White. Rising above a Toxic Workplace: Taking Care of Yourself in an Unhealthy Environment. Northfield Publishing, 2014.
- Crail, C. (2023, July 13). 15 effective employee retention strategies in 2023. Forbes. https://www.forbes.com/advisor/business/employee-retention-strategies/
- Durré, Linnda. Surviving the Toxic Workplace: Protect Yourself against Coworkers, Bosses, and Work Environments That Poison Your Day. Nota, 2022.
- Indeed. (2023, February 23). 13 effective employee retention strategies - indeed. 13 Effective Retention Strategies. https://www.indeed.com/hire/c/info/9-effective-employee-retention-strategies
- Hansen, Kris. "Ideal Reader Questionnaire." One City United, Aug. 2023.
- MacLellan, Lila. "At Patagonia, Exit Interviews Are Rare-but They Go Deep." Quartz, Quartz, 20 Mar. 2019, qz.com/work/1574375.
- Rising Strong by Brené Brown. Daily Books, 2015. www.audible.com

- Samuel Stebbins, Evan Comen. "The Worst Cities for Black Americans." 24/7 Wall St., 11 Jan. 2020, 247wallst.com/special-report/2018/11/09/the-worst-cities-for-black-americans-4/.
- Ramsey Solutions. (2023, February 23). 5 employee Retention Strategies Your Business Needs. https://www.ramseysolutions.com/business/employee-retention#5-employee-retention-strategies-your-business-needs-right-now 5 Employee Retention Strategies Your Business Needs Right Now
- Skipper, Jeff, et al. "How to Improve Employee Retention (5 Steps) - Business Leadership Today." Business Leadership Today - The Resource for Leaders Working to Build and Sustain World-Class Teams and Organizations in Today's Business Environment., 2 Oct. 2023, businessleadershiptoday.com/how-to-improve-employee-retention/.
- Slack. (2023, February 23). 5 employee retention strategies every company should implement. https://slack.com/blog/transformation/employee-retention-strategies
- "Stigma." Oxford Language.
- Stoewen, Debbie L. "Dimensions of Wellness: Change Your Habits, Change Your Life." The Canadian Veterinary Journal = La Revue Veterinaire Canadienne, U.S. National Library of Medicine, Aug. 2017, www.ncbi.nlm.nih.gov/pmc/articles/PMC5508938/.
- "15 Effective Employee Retention Strategies in 2024." Forbes, Forbes Magazine, 10 May 2024, www.forbes.com/advisor/business/employee-retention-strategies/.
- "6 Effective Employee Retention Strategies for 2023." Workhuman, 19 Oct. 2023, www.workhuman.com/blog/effective-employee-retention-strategies/.
- "6 Effective Employee Retention Strategies for 2023." Workhuman, 19 Oct. 2023, www.workhuman.com/blog/effective-employee-retention-strategies/.
- "6 Effective Employee Retention Strategies for 2023." Workhuman, 19 Oct. 2023, www.workhuman.com/blog/effective-employee-retention-strategies/.
- "About." Iowa Peer Workforce Collaborative - The University of Iowa, iowapeersupport.sites.uiowa.edu/about. Accessed 3 Sept. 2024.

- "Brené Brown on Our Current 'B.A.D' (Badass Deficit) - a Clip from One of the Many New Films Coming Soon with Brené.: By the Work of the Peoplefacebook." Facebook, Oct. 2015, www.facebook.com/theworkofthepeople/videos/bren%C3%A9-brown-on-our-current-bad-badass-deficit-a-clip-from-one-of-the-many-new-fi/10153628706010682/.
- Brown, Brene', and Eric Mosley. "Brené with Eric Mosley on Making Work Human." Brené with Eric Mosley on Making Work Human, 17 Jan. 2024, brenebrown.com/podcast/brene-with-eric-mosley-on-making-work-human/.
- Brown, Brene'. "Chapter 12/Dehumanization." Atlas Of The Heart, Mapping Meaningful Connection and the Language of Human Experience, Random House, 2021, pp. 233–235.
- Chapman, Gary D., and Paul E. White. Rising above a Toxic Workplace: Taking Care of Yourself in an Unhealthy Environment. Northfield Publishing, 2014.
- Durré, Linnda. Surviving the Toxic Workplace: Protect Yourself against Coworkers, Bosses, and Work Environments That Poison Your Day. Nota, 2022.
- "Fix the Damn Roof." YouTube, YouTube, www.youtube.com/results?search_query=Fix%2Bthe%2BDamn%2BRoof%2BTed%2B Talk. Accessed 26 Aug. 2024.
- MacLellan, Lila. "At Patagonia, Exit Interviews Are Rare-but They Go Deep." Quartz, Quartz, 20 Mar. 2019, qz.com/work/1574375.
- "The Reckoning. ." Rising Strong by Brené Brown, Daily Books, 2017, www.audiblebooks.com.
- Rising Strong by Brené Brown. Daily Books, 2015.
- Samuel Stebbins, Evan Comen. "The Worst Cities for Black Americans." 24/7 Wall St., 11 Jan. 2020, 247wallst.com/special-report/2018/11/09/the-worst-cities-for-black-americans-4/.
- SHRM Getting Talent Back to Work Report, 2021.
- SHRM Getting Talent Back to Work Report, 2021.
- Skipper, Jeff, et al. "How to Improve Employee Retention (5 Steps) - Business Leadership Today." Business Leadership Today - The Resource for Leaders Working to Build and Sustain World-Class Teams and Organizations in Today's Business Environment., 2 Oct. 2023, businessleadershiptoday.com/how-to-improve-employee-retention/.
- "Stigma." Oxford Language.

- Stoewen, Debbie L. "Dimensions of Wellness: Change Your Habits, Change Your Life." The Canadian Veterinary Journal = La Revue Veterinaire Canadienne, U.S. National Library of Medicine, Aug. 2017, www.ncbi.nlm.nih.gov/pmc/articles/PMC5508938/.
- Thomas C. Frohlich, Sam Stebbins. "The Worst Cities for Black Americans." 24/7 Wall St., 4 Dec. 2019, 247wallst.com/special-report/2015/10/06/the-worst-cities-for-black-americans/?tpid=2919 13&tv=link&tc=in_content.
- "Turnipseed Trilogy." YouTube, youtu.be/KmDU6qILxPc?si=jM-G5ReN6PsJJJRC. Accessed 26 Aug. 2024.
- Turnipseed, Johnny. "Fix the Damn Roof." TED TALK Fix The Damn Roof, YouTube, 6 Aug. 2012, www.youtube.com/watch?v=sL3Ntcb50wA.
- Wagner, Wendy Sawyer and Peter. "Mass Incarceration: The Whole Pie 2024." Prison Policy Initiative, www.prisonpolicy.org/reports/pie2024.html. Accessed 25 Aug. 2024.
- Ways to Engage Community Partners, Https:// Themanufacturinginstitute.Org/Workers/Second-Chance/ Building-Community-Partnerships/#IDENTIFYING, https:// themanufacturinginstitute.org/workers/second-chance/building-community-partnerships/#IDENTIFYING.
- West, Schad. "Ideal Reader Questionare." One City United , Aug. 2023.
- "Workplace Supported Recovery." Centers for Disease Control and Prevention, Centers for Disease Control and Prevention, 21 Dec. 2023, www.cdc.gov/niosh/substance-use/workplace-supported-recovery/index.html.
- YouTube, Turnipseed Trilogy, youtu.be/KmDU6qILxPc?si=jM-G5ReN6PsJJJRC. Accessed 26 Aug. 2024.
- YouTube, YouTube, www.youtube.com/results?search_query=Fix%2 Bthe%2BDamn%2BRoof%2BTed%2BTalk. Accessed 27 Aug. 2024.

Thank You!

**Sending a special Thank You to
One City United's Board Members (*Past & Present*)**

Your dedication to filling gaps & equipping people
has impacted and transformed lives!

I appreciate you!

Dean Feltes,

One City United Executive Director

~~~~~~~~~~

Phil Akin

Lisa Ambrose

Timi Brown-Powers

Rick Bauer

Jenny Boevers

Ruth Cole

Joe Fox

Debra Hodges-Harmon

Jim Horton

Holly Johnson

Chiquita Loveless

Mary McKinnell

Lynn Neill

Jordan Nomansen

Lauren Nomansen

Heather Roby

Walt Rogers

Jay Schmitz

Stephanie Shavers

Bill Tate

Chris Wendland

Schad West

One City United staff:

Supportive Service Coordinator: Alicia Wilder
Classroom Coordinator: Robin Smith
Technology Coordinator & Recovery Coach: Riley Scheetz
Peer Support Coach: Ashley Schneider, BSW

Master's in Social Work Intern:

Alexis Harris

Recovery Coach Interns:

Brandy Caldwell, Dustin Dawson & Sabrina Little

Thank you to all who have made the wheels turn and have poured into the lives of our Momentum classes for the past four years:

- Aysha Weekley: Target Corporation
- Abraham Funchess: Waterloo Human Rights
- Alex Covarrubias: Western Home Communities Talent Acquisition Specialist
- Alexis Feltes: Happy Time Daycare, Women of Strength Founder
- Amber McLaughlin: Former OCU staff
- Amber McNeeley: Student, Momentum inspiration for change
- Amie Buckley: Riverview Center
- Amy Eastman: Viking Pump/IDEX Corporation
- Angela Wunder: John Deere
- Annie VanderWerff: GTA Consulting
- Ashley Caldwell: Ashley Speaks & Tri County Head Start
- Arlen Yost: Cedar Valley Bridge of Hope
- Becky Weaver: Bossard Corporation
- Bill Tate: Retired PO Department of Corrections, former One City Board Member
- Bob Lincoln: Elevate CCBHC Founder/Project Director
- Brooke Kraft: VGM Corporation Talent Acquisition
- Candace Yount: Olive Garden Waterloo
- Charlie Barfels: CPM Corporation
- Chassidy Martin: Royal Legacy Christian Academy Co-Founder
- Chatara Mabry: Professor of Social Work
- Chiquita Loveless: One Cedar Valley, University of Northern Iowa, Former One City United Board Member

- Chris Nicholas: To Work Coordinator
- Christopher Schwartz: Black Hawk County Supervisor
- Christy Decker: Dupaco Community Credit Union
- Chol Chagai: Mercy One Hospital Head of Dietary Department
- Conner Erickson: Hy-Vee Store Manager Crossroads Waterloo
- Darcey Birch: City & National Employment
- Dan Trelka: Retired Police Chief/Black Hawk County Supervisor
- Danielle McGeough: University of Northern Iowa Communication Dept.
- Daniel Shafer: Catholic Charities
- Deon Harris: Author and Founder of Progress Platform Publications LLC
- Debra Harmon: Jessie Cosby Executive Director/ Former OCU Board Member
- Devin Mahaffey: Reform
- Donna Peterson: Love INC. A great cheerleader!
- Doug Marshall: Retired Iowa Works / Board of Iowa Justice Action Network
- Dr. Joyce Levingston: YWCA Executive Director/ Former OCU Staff
- Dr. Quinton Richardson with Iowa State Extension
- Elana Reader: Tyson's Corporation
- Felicia Carter: Pathways / Center of Attention
- Gabrielle Fleischhacker: Hawkeye Community College Peer Gap Education
- Gina Weekley: Leader Valley / Waterloo Schools
- Glen Keith: Love INC., Executive Director
- Heather Peiffer: Cedar Valley Hospice / Waterloo Schools
- Heather Robinson: Durham Bus
- Jamie Caesar: Mercy One Hospital Human Resource
- Jason Higham: Dirty Work LLC
- Jason Kastli: UnityPoint Health EVS
- Jay Schmitz: Viking Pump/IDEX Corporation
- Jayne Hall: Community Bank & Trust Community Relations and Development
- Jennifer Becker, LISW: Director of Field Instruction University of Northern Iowa
- Jennifer Boevers: Nurse UnityPoint Health /Former OCU Board Member
- Jennifer Oliver: UnityPoint Health Human Resource Recruiter
- Jim Dick: Retired High School Superintendent

- Jim Horton: Retired Caterpillar Executive / OCU Board Member
- Jodie Hill : UnityPoint Health EVS Department
- Joe Fox: Owner Fox Enterprises LLC/
  Former OCU Board Member
- Joe Trumbley: Elevate CCBHC BSW Substance Use Counselor
- Joelle Murray: Oak Park Assisted Living
- Jonathan Griedner: Waterloo Schools
- Jordan Dunn: Counselor/HR Pathways CCBHC
- Joseph Austin: Former OCU staff
- Joy Briscoe: Executive Director One Cedar Valley/ 24/7 BLAC
- Julia Bisbey-Kuehn: Kay Park & Recreation
- Karen Rowe: House of Hope Executive Director
- Katy Susong: Cardinal Construction
- Kevin McCollough: Cedar Falls Furniture Mart Store Manager
- Keya Jackson: Kay Park & Recreation
- Kim Kalthoff: Inclusion Connection Job Developer & Job Coach
- Kingsley Botchway II: UnityPoint Health Human Resource
- Kirby Sanders: Target Corporation
- Kyle Horn: America's Job Honor Awards
- Kyle Roed: CPM Corporation International Human Resource
- Larry Lavenz: VGM Corporation
- Latoya Godfrey: Amani Service Director/ One City Outreach
- Laura Yeats: Cedar Valley Hospice
- Lisa Ambrose: Amani Service Founder
  /Former OCU Board Member
- Liz Blair: Entrepreneur, educator
- Lori Dale: Hawkeye Community College student
- Luis Couvertier: Isle Casino Security
- Lynn Neill: Retired Social Worker / OCU Board Member
- Mark Sherburne: Kay Park & Recreation, Plant Manager
- Marshall Wade: Former OCU To Work Driver
- Mary Dick: Retired PO/ Educator, Central Community College in Rockwell City Prison
- Marshall Wade: Former OCU staff
- Mary McKinnell : Executive Director County Social Services/ OCU Board of Directors
- Maura McNamara: Northeast Iowa Food Bank
- Maurice Davis: Jayne Boyd, Cedar Rapids
- Mayor Danny Laudick: Cedar Falls
- Mayor Quentin Hart: Waterloo
- Megan Hartwig: Kay Park & Recreation Human Resource

- Mel Amoni: Elevate CCBHC, IRSH Program Coach
- Melissa Card: Human Resources Power Engineering & Manufacturing, Ltd.
- Michael Menton: CPM Corporation
- Mikhayla Gramlich: Pathways CCBHC Peer Support/ Student HCC
- Micheal Anderson: Pathways, HCC Student
- Michael Menton: CPM Corporation
- Michele Rutledge: Healthcare CNA
- Michelle Meaney: Community Bank and Trust, Branch Manager
- Nancy Steinbron: Dignity Apparel
- Nia Wilder: Spark Lot owner, & Waterloo City Councilwoman
- Nicholas Rosauer: UnityPoint Health, Manager Behavioral Health Services
- Nicole Litzel: Iowa Works
- Nick Barnett: Domestic Dad Project
- Nikki Carrion: Wellness Educator
- Paige Eddy: UnityPoint EVS
- Pastor Chad Adelmund: Heartland Community Church
- Pastor Charles Daniel: Antioch Church
- Pastor Del Rittgers: Evansdale Hope Church of the Nazarene
- Pastor Shane Blackledge: Celebrate Recovery, Author
- Ron Protsman: Community Outreach
- Rev. Dr. Frantz Whitfield: Mt Carmel Church
- Rev. Dr. Marshaundus Robinson: Impact Church of Hope
- Rev. Rudy Jones: City of Waterloo Community Development
- Pastor William Campbell: Cathedral of Faith Church
- Purvis Williams: Project Ready and REM
- Raechel Miller: Northeast Iowa Food Bank
- Randall Carlson: Western Home Communities Hospitality Director
- Raquel Ita: VGM Corporation Fulfillment Director of People & Culture
- Rebbeca Johnson: Waterloo Human Rights
- Reshonda Young: Bank of Jabez, Entrepreneur, Sister Friends Podcast
- Rev. Brian Dale: St. Marks Missionary Baptist
- Rev. Dr. City Councilwoman Belinda Creighton-Smith
- Rick Yount: Caseys Denver Manager
- Robert Ackermann: Mercy One Hospital/ Former One City To Work staff

- Rob Nichols: Greenwood Pharmacy, Pharmacist & Waterloo City Councilperson
- Ryan Nesbit: Alive and Running Founder
- Ryan Stevenson: Self Employed, Stevenson Group
- Ruth Cole: PTO CREATOR / OCU Board Member
- Sandin Hadziric: Mercy One Hospital
- Schad West: Kay Park Recreation Operations Manager/OCU Board Member
- Shanterra Martin: Community Bank & Trust, Branch Manager
- Sherman Wise: Premiere Staffing
- Stacey & Jeffrey Springer: Community Outreach
- Stephanie Shavers: Neighborhood Services City of Waterloo
- Steve Stats: Cedar Valley Bridge of Hope
- Stephen Kroger: EMCOR Building Maintenance

- Tanara Wade: Waterloo Schools and Former OCU staff
- Tami Adelmund: VGM Corporation
- Teresa Culpepper: Hawkeye Community College Nursing Educator
- Theresa Steiber-Community Outreach
- Tim Diesburg: Retired Iowa Prison Industries Apprenticeship Supervisor
- Thomas Kullen: Elevate CBHCC Peer Support Specialist
- Troy Midthus: CPM Corporation
- Urban Alliance 2018 Team: Luke, Brian, Chris, and Esto
- Vera Wallican: Child Protection Policy Program Manager, IA Dep. HHS / Celebrate Sisterhood Founder
- Vicki Jones: Upper Iowa University
- Zachary Garrigus: VGM Operations Manager
- Zac Mitchell: Former To Work Driver, Waterloo Schools, Author

I sincerely apologize if I missed your name.

Made in the USA
Columbia, SC
12 February 2025

53675137R00089